THE SUNDAY TIMES

Boost Your Self-Esteem

D0047298

John Caunt

△ KOGAN PAGE | *CREATING SUCCESS*

First published in 2003
Reprinted 2003

Kogan Page Limited
120 Pentonville Road
London N1 9JN

www.kogan-page.co.uk

British Library Cataloguing in Publication Data

A CIP record for this book is available from the British Library.

ISBN 0 7494 3871 1

Typeset by Jean Cussons Typesetting, Diss, Norfolk
Printed and bound in Great Britain by Clays Ltd, St Ives plc

contents

introduction

Self-esteem is about the value we place on ourselves. It is the fundamental assessment we make of our own worth as human beings. It is affected by the extent to which we consider we are living our lives according to our aspirations and standards and also by the actions and reactions of other people towards us. And it's important. Feeling good about ourselves not only means greater enjoyment from life, it can impact greatly on our performance in everything we do. But for many of us, our estimation of self-worth is not as high as we would wish. We experience feelings of inferiority, self-doubt and anxiety. Such limitations on our self-esteem may mean that we:

- stay in the comfort zone avoiding new experiences;
- torture ourselves with doubts about our capabilities;
- fail to assert ourselves when the situation demands;
- gain only fleeting satisfaction from our successes;
- feel that we are not in control of situations;
- punish ourselves or blame others for our misfortunes rather than taking responsibility for change;
- expend energy comparing ourselves with others and resenting their success.

Developing greater self-esteem means being:

- more at ease and in control of situations;
- able to bounce back from failures and disappointments;
- positive and optimistic in our expectations of ourselves and others;
- able to act independently without being overly reliant on the views of others;
- ready to stand up for ourselves when the need arises;
- prepared to take on new challenges without being wracked by fear and worry about how things might turn out;
- honest and open with ourselves and others.

In short, it means a much better chance of getting the best out of ourselves and out of life.

are there benefits to low self-esteem?

There is a tendency for us to regard modesty and mild self-deprecation as rather nice traits – the opposite end of the scale from boastfulness and excessive self-regard. And if this is the case, we might go on to argue that a certain amount of low self-esteem is not a bad thing – helps us keep this rough old world in perspective, not expecting too much and not getting above ourselves. It's tempting to use this argument to justify continued self-deprecation. But it really doesn't wash. High self-esteem does not have to mean boastfulness and arrogance. You can still be modest about your achievements; in fact you may be more so because you don't feel the need to prove yourself to others or seek their approval. Many of those who appear boastful and arrogant are presenting an inflated image of themselves for public consumption precisely because it matters to them what other people think. They may need the pretence that pomposity offers to cover their own feelings of inadequacy.

A second argument in favour of low self-esteem might be that feelings of inferiority can be a guard against complacency, leading us to strive harder for success. It's true that for some people the drive to succeed comes from feelings of low self-worth, but this type of fuel offers a bumpy ride through life – limited enjoyment of the ups and despondency when faced with the inevitable downs. Far healthier is the drive that comes from a positive view of one's own worth linked to a clear sense of direction.

who suffers from low self-esteem?

Most of us, at some time in our lives, will experience some degree of diminished self-esteem. The range extends from those whose self-belief is only rocked by severe stress or major life crises, to those who doubt themselves at all times and in all circumstances. But it is a rare individual whose self-esteem is so strong that it can survive all conceivable onslaughts. And difficulties are not confined to those who display the more obvious signs of depression and anxiety. Indeed, it is a paradox of self-esteem that it frequently dogs those who by any objective measure would be considered among the most assured and successful. You may be outwardly confident, clearly able to cope with all the demands of life, and yet still suffer from that sense that you are a fraud, a failure, not worthy enough.

While few of us are immune from damage, those with a long-established low self-image have more sensitive antennae and will be less able to weather the brickbats of life. It's also the case that people with low self-esteem tend to be seen as easy targets by those seeking to counter their own feelings of inadequacy by controlling others. But the good news is that we can do something about it, and in the forthcoming chapters we will explore the strategies you can use to make a difference. We will look at how to shift negative thinking about yourself and establish a greater sense of self-worth. We will consider how to deal with the threats to self-esteem that may come from other people or the setbacks we encounter in life. And we will examine ways to achieve an improved sense of direction and balance in your life.

This is a book aimed at anyone who feels their life is less fulfilling than it might be because of an element of negativity in the view they have of themselves. So, does that include you? To get an idea, consider whether any of the following statements in Table 0.1 apply.

If you answer 'never' to every one of these, then you are either fooling yourself or you have no need of this book. For everybody else, read on, there is something here for you.

the Creating Success series

The *Sunday Times* Creating Success series deals primarily with workplace issues. Healthy levels of self-esteem are clearly important to your performance and sense of fulfilment at work, but any attempt to confine the subject matter of this book purely to work-related situations would risk a distorted and inadequate treatment. So, while I have used a number of workplace examples, and have given some attention to particular issues such as work–life balance, the book remains one that deals with the whole person, and should be of value to anyone wishing to raise levels of self-esteem regardless of their circumstances.

Table 0.1 *Self-esteem checklist*

	Always	Sometimes	Never
I feel guilty about asking others for help.			
I get upset by criticism.			
If I can't do something well, I feel there is no point in doing it at all.			
I need someone to point out if I have done a good job.			
I feel undeserving of other people's time and attention.			
When I suffer failure, I experience fundamental doubts about my abilities.			
I feel the need to prove myself.			
There are times when I don't like myself.			
I expect more of myself than I would of others.			
I avoid new friendships and relationships for fear of rejection.			
I tend to be rather self-critical.			
I worry about the way things may turn out.			
I doubt my ability to achieve what I want.			
I compare myself unfavourably with others.			
I avoid disagreements.			
I think of myself as a failure.			
I fear that I will be unable to handle difficult situations.			
I resent others who appear more successful than me.			
I give inadequate attention to my physical and emotional well-being.			
I fear making a fool of myself.			
There are times when I make myself feel better at the expense of others.			

understand the problem

foundations

Self-esteem is first and foremost a product of our experiences in childhood and adolescence. During that crucial period when we are making sense of the world around us, all manner of influences impact on us that may give rise to negative views of ourselves. The people wielding the influence are those whose opinions matter most to us – parents, siblings, peers, teachers. As we move through from childhood into adolescence, the views of our peers assume increased importance and those of the adult figures may diminish. There is a host of different ways in which self-esteem can be damaged. Here are just a few of them:

 receiving conditional affection – 'I only like/love you if... ';
 being on the receiving end of threatening or abusive behaviour;
 overprotection, particularly if it is made clear that the reason for such treatment is your weakness or inability to look after yourself;

▓ excessive criticism, ridicule, humiliation;

▓ ostracism from the group because you don't fit in, perhaps by reason of physical, social or behavioural differences;

▓ being required to follow activities unsuited to your talents – eg a non-sporting child being thrust into a regime of physical exercise and competitive games;

▓ being compared unfavourably with more successful peers or siblings;

▓ growing up in a family where low self-esteem is the norm;

▓ being encouraged to pay too much attention to what other people may think;

▓ being presented with unrealistic expectations of achievement.

While the foundations of our self-esteem or lack of it are normally laid down in childhood, it continues to be bruised and battered when we are adults. It may be subject to threat when we are:

▓ rejected, overlooked or taken for granted;

▓ deceived or taken for a ride;

▓ on the receiving end of unfair criticism or put-downs;

▓ made aware of shortcomings in our skills or knowledge;

▓ conscious that we have failed to live up to our own ideals;

▓ bullied, harassed or abused;

▓ subject to excessive stress;

▓ enduring negative life events – relationship difficulties, periods of unemployment, bereavement.

It is important to recognise that the view we have of ourselves is simply a collection of impressions and opinions that we have reached on the basis of experiences we go through and our perceptions of other people's responses to us. But, while the consequences of some of these experiences can be profound, there exists no inevitable cause and effect relationship. Any of the experiences in the above lists may lead to a diminution in self-belief, but they do so because we allow them to. What is more, we are inclined to introduce distortions into the way we think about our experiences and our capacity for dealing with them.

distortions of perception

■ We misperceive our own performance at times of stress. When we are feeling under pressure it is easy to reach erroneous conclusions about our own behaviour. Quite wrongly we decide that we've blundered, made fools of ourselves, not behaved as we would have wished.

■ We misinterpret the responses of others. Over-sensitivity to the reactions of others leads us to attribute motives that are not present, find criticism where it wasn't intended and interpret anything less than unconditional praise as rejection.

■ Other people misjudge us and let their own insecurities get in the way of their reactions to us. We fail to recognise that their reactions may be coloured by the anxiety, jealousy or stress they are experiencing.

distortions of invention

■ We reach conclusions about ourselves on the basis of very limited evidence. One or two examples may be elevated into a general rule, which we then apply at all times.

■ We put the worst possible construction on events, and reach wholly insupportable conclusions about our own lack of worth.

▓ We feel a sense of blame for problems that were not
our fault.

▓ We exaggerate our flaws and weaknesses.

distortions of omission

▓ We ignore any evidence that contradicts the negative
view we hold of ourselves.

▓ We refuse to give ourselves credit for our positive qualities.

▓ We disregard our achievements.

distortions of prediction

▓ We overstate the likelihood that things will go wrong.

▓ We exaggerate the likely consequences of failure.

▓ We underestimate our abilities to deal with problems.

Given that we suffer all these distortions as adults, consider
how much more potent they were at the time we were just
learning to make sense of our world and the other people that
inhabit it. Parental criticism was so much more hurtful at the
time when we still believed our parents to be infallible, a bully's
behaviour more damaging when we hadn't yet realised that he
or she was a sad loser.

So, we arrive at a set of fundamental negative conclusions
about ourselves – the result of experiences we have had and
distortions we have introduced – and may adopt a variety of
coping strategies aimed at protecting ourselves from the pain of
confronting these negative beliefs. Four common strategies
could be described as withdrawing, counter-attacking, deferring or resigning, and controlling.

withdrawing

One way we may deal with the fundamental negative beliefs we
hold about ourselves is to avoid the situations in which there is

a perceived risk of being hurt or exposed. Those who adopt this approach may put up barriers to stop others getting close to them, or steer clear of challenges they expect will lead to failure and expose their inadequacy. The consequence is that they will miss out on many of the more satisfying experiences that life has to offer.

> *Andrea*: Andrea was a shy and sensitive only child of nine when her father died suddenly. Her mother's subsequent remarriage was to a man who already had three children and Andrea felt herself to be the outsider in this new larger family, particularly as she perceived her step-brother and sisters to be more talented and outgoing than she was. She interpreted as rejection her mother's attempts to give equal care and affection to all four children and came to view her step-siblings' successes as confirmation of her own lack of worth. As an adult she so fears the pain and humiliation of failure and rejection that she avoids any experiences that involve risk – be they new relationships, unfamiliar social situations or new career challenges. She remains firmly within her comfort zone and, starved of opportunities to learn and grow, her low self-esteem is endlessly confirmed.

counter-attacking

Rather than folding under the perceived weight of their inadequacy, some people respond by turning their lives into a series of challenges. Their subconscious rationale is that only by overcoming the obstacles they place in their own way can they feel good about themselves. Often the goals set are unrealistic and objectives not achieved bring despondency and confirmation of the low opinion they have of themselves. Ironically, when such individuals do achieve success they tend to downgrade the importance of it or attribute it to a fluke rather than their own hard work or ability. So the very goals they are striving towards are ultimately unsatisfying when achieved.

Trevor: Trevor was a bright child whose family moved from their native Wales to the Home Counties just as he was about to start at secondary school. He did not make friends easily in the new environment and suffered playground ridicule on account of his Welsh accent. He was also self-conscious about his family's economic circumstances, which were less favourable than those of most of his peers and, as a rather weedy child, he was on the receiving end of some physical bullying. He developed a sense of inferiority, which he carried through into adulthood, but compensated for this by setting himself challenges – work, sport etc – by which he could prove his worth and gain the acceptance he felt he needed. He achieved success in a demanding career and developed a wide range of social, sporting and leisure interests. However, his constant need to prove himself continues to generate a great deal of anxiety. Whenever his performance is below his self-imposed high standards, it serves to confirm the poor view he has of himself, and even success fails to give him the satisfaction he craves. While he would be ready to attribute the successes of others to ability or hard work, he regards his own as a matter of chance. Inside, he feels himself to be a fraud.

---

deferring

Those who take this line are inclined to subjugate their own wants and feelings to those of others. They will passively go along with more forceful individuals, avoiding confrontation or any action that might upset people. But their passivity does not necessarily imply contentment. They may feel a great deal of anger, directed at themselves as well as anyone they perceive to have damaged them, but they consider themselves powerless to change matters. They are resigned to their feelings of worthlessness and will heap self-condemnation on top of that which they feel they have received from others.

Ann: Ann went from a childhood marked by demanding and critical parents into an early marriage to a domineering husband. Somewhere along the line she came to the view that the route to love and acceptance lay in pleasing others and putting their needs ahead of her own. She lets it be known by word and action that her views and opinions count for very little, and she has a horror of any form of disagreement. Nevertheless, she is conscious that her strategy of constantly deferring to others does not bring the desired results, and her failure ever to assert herself is a further source of damage to her self-esteem.

controlling

Instead of surrendering control as in the previous example, a fourth strand of behaviour might be attempting to deal with one's low self-belief by seeking excessive control over one's environment. This might involve bullying, manipulative or other controlling behaviour towards others, or it might take the form of excessive planning and organisation, nit-picking over detail or a tendency towards perfectionism.

Edward: Distorted perceptions of his own behaviour in a variety of situations have left Edward with an underlying belief that he is an incompetent buffoon. His response to this fundamental negative view is to make sure that he is never in a position where his incompetence is exposed, and in pursuit of this he seeks perfection in everything he does or is associated with. He plans obsessively and spends a great deal of time and energy worrying about the things that might go wrong. At work he is loath to delegate tasks to others and, when he has to do so, he constantly interferes with their execution to ensure they are done precisely to his wishes. He feels threatened by views that differ from his own, and is known to throw tantrums when he is in danger of not getting his own way.

Edward only feels good about himself when he meets his ideal of perfection – a situation patently impossible to maintain constantly. When he falls short of his standards, it serves to confirm the fundamental negative belief he has about himself. Furthermore, there are many tasks and challenges he won't even embark upon because he fears that he won't be able to do them perfectly, and these instil a further sense of inadequacy and failure.

The above examples are, of course, simplifications. As such they miss the nuances and infinite variety that make us such complex and interesting creatures. We may display combinations of these traits and more besides, and we shift our behaviour according to circumstance. I hope, however, that they serve to illustrate some of the strategies we adopt to deal with long-standing lack of self-belief. Such strategies become ingrained habits that may be everyday features of our behaviour or called into play when we face particularly challenging situations. But, as we have seen, the strategies create their own stresses and may lead to a vicious circle of self-deprecation that feeds and sustains the initial low self-esteem.

I'm not going to pretend that long-standing habits are simple to change. It will require some effort and commitment, but you can change them. The steps towards making a difference are as follows:

1. Recognise and admit to the presence of the destructive habit.
2. Be clear about the benefits that will come from changing your behaviour and the damage presently caused by the habit.
3. Tackle the root causes of the behaviour – the fundamental negative beliefs you have about yourself.
4. Believe in your ability to make the change.

5. Set yourself staged targets for change – ie behaving differently in certain situations or with particular people.
6. Build on your successes and set new targets.
7. Reward yourself for every step forward you take.
8. Stick with it. There will be times when it seems you have slipped backwards. But a setback does not mean that you have failed.

We will explore some of these themes further in subsequent chapters.

attaching strings

For most of us there is a strong link between our self-belief and our perceptions of how we are doing in terms of relationships, social situations, employment, health and appearance. Do we look good? Do people like us? Are we doing well at work? We make a positive self-image conditional upon things going well for us in these various areas. To an extent, this is not an unhealthy thing. Our successes and the reactions of others are legitimate ingredients in the way we feel about ourselves; they encourage us to overcome new challenges and to continue to give of our best. But they become unhealthy when the condition is elevated to overriding importance – when we say to ourselves, 'I can only feel good about myself if... ':

■ I can only feel good about myself if I am slim.
■ I can only feel good about myself if I am receiving praise and reassurance.
■ I can only feel good about myself if I achieve perfection in the things I set out to do.

Whenever we attribute excessive importance to achievement in certain aspects of our lives, we present ourselves with a problem. Clearly, it is not possible for us always to enjoy success, and the occasions when we are suffering setbacks are those when we most need healthy self-esteem. But when self-belief is pinned to the very thing that is going badly – and when the reason for the setback may be beyond our control – we are faced with a very difficult recovery task.

Larry: Larry's self-esteem was pinned to success at work. After some early setbacks, he was able to obtain a job where he felt his talents were recognised. He progressed rapidly through the ranks of junior management and, although he never lost a deep-seated sense of uncertainty about his merits, he was able to shield himself from the discomfort this caused him by immersing himself in his position and his status as a successful manager. His work became his defining identity and everything else – relationships, leisure, personal development – took second place. When, through no fault of his, Larry was made redundant, the whole edifice collapsed and he was left at rock bottom.

Ruth: Ruth's self-esteem is heavily dependent on how she feels about her appearance. As with so many of us, she compares herself unfavourably with the glossy examples of supposedly perfect humanity that appear in the media. She is neither overweight nor unattractive, but tends to exaggerate her perceived flaws out of all proportion. A minor skin blemish or a little extra weight in the wrong place becomes, in her mind, a reason for others to shun her company completely. She suffers a double burden – striving after an artificial and unattainable ideal, and imposing upon herself an exceptionally harsh assessment of her own appearance.

There is no denying that we all feel better about ourselves if we are happy about the way we look, but to pin too much self-belief on to appearance is to condemn yourself to some pretty nasty dips. By all means spend effort on your appearance and presentation, but keep it within reason. And most importantly, don't forget that real attractiveness is not an external thing. People who tell themselves, 'If I were more attractive I would believe in myself' may be approaching the issue from the wrong direction. What perhaps they should be saying is, 'If I believed in myself I would be more attractive.' Research has shown that attributes like confidence, warmth and social skills can be far more influential in how we are perceived by those we would like to know, than simply the way we look.

removing strings

OK. Allowing our self-esteem to be excessively dependent on particular strengths, achievements or accolades is potentially damaging. So what is the alternative? It has to be about taking hold of a greater unconditional regard for ourselves – getting rid of the notion that perceived shortcomings make us in some way less worthwhile. Regardless of what you do, how you look, what others may say about you, you are of equal worth and as deserving of equal respect as everyone else on the planet. If you are inclined to pin too much of your self-esteem on to certain conditions, it's time to start liking yourself just for being you. Think about other people you love or have loved unconditionally – a partner, a special friend, your children. You don't expect them to be perfect; your love for them doesn't diminish when they fall short of some particular ideal. You can be pleased and proud of their successes, but their achievements are not the basis on which your love for them is founded.

The benefits of a greater unconditional element to self-esteem are easy to see. A stronger underlying sense of one's own value means that setbacks, criticism and rejection will have less effect. They will not plunge you into the pit of worthlessness. I'm not suggesting that you seek to develop the sort of ghastly bombproof self-adulation that one encounters from time to time – simply that you redress the balance somewhat. Self-esteem will always be to a degree dependent on praise and achievement, but whatever the ups and downs of your experience you will remain worthy of love and respect – most particularly from yourself.

competence and self-esteem

As we have already seen in one of the earlier examples, there is no automatic link between one's competence and the level of one's self-esteem. Many highly competent people suffer grave doubts about themselves. To others they may be recognised as able and successful, but they perceive themselves to be failures. Very often there is a sense of being a fraud – that success has only been acquired by chance – and that there is an ever-present danger of being rumbled with all the consequent exposure and humiliation. Praise is dismissed on the grounds that it comes from people who are unaware of the individual's fundamental flaws and, were they aware of the fraudulent nature of the individual's success, they would surely withdraw their approval. Similarly, achievements bring little in the way of satisfaction. The fact that they were attained by such a flawed individual means that they cannot count for very much. People who suffer from this difficulty can find themselves in the paradoxical situation where long sought-after objectives, once attained, lose their significance. There is a sense of anticlimax and a feeling that the objective must have been spurious in some way.

what to do about it

The first step in dealing with the problem is to recognise that you are not the only one who suffers from it. It is pretty common among high-achieving individuals and may well be growing. In the modern work environment in particular, skills and competencies are changing so rapidly that it is easy to feel that you have missed out somewhere along the line – that you have failed to grasp some important skill. The amount of information we are required to handle means that nobody can know everything. The degree of pressure and the levels of sophistication are so great that even the most competent can feel that they are hanging on by their fingertips. Everyone may be struggling, but there is frequently a culture in which owning up to one's difficulties is not done. Instead, everyone carries on bluffing it out.

Ask yourself some questions:

1. What are the fraudulent aspects of myself that I think I am currently hiding?
2. Are they valid? Are they genuine deficiencies or the result of distorted thinking?
3. If they are real deficiencies, am I guilty of exaggerating their importance or my uniqueness in possessing them?
4. Are my predictions of what would happen if I revealed these weaknesses valid? What is really the worst that could happen?

Clear out the distorted thinking and the exaggerated predictions, and don't be so tough on yourself. Recognise that you cannot be equally expert in all you do. We all have areas of weakness. Allow yourself to admit to not knowing, to being a beginner in some things. It will seldom result in the predicted ridicule. In fact, the person who admits to their shortcomings and is prepared to learn is generally more highly regarded than the one who blunders through with bluff and cover-up.

2

put yourself in the driving seat

Our self-esteem can be strongly influenced by how much we perceive ourselves to be in control of our lives. Do we have authority over our actions and reactions to people and situations? Do we have a sense of direction and the ability to will the means of arriving at where we want to be? Can we control our own fears and anxieties, the tendency to punish ourselves? Or are we being helplessly swept along – the victims of every snub and setback – clinging on to recrimination and lost aspirations?

This theme of control will be a recurring one throughout the book, and I would like to kick off in this chapter with a brief consideration of the ways in which we can get rid of excess baggage from the past and over-dependence on others in the present.

discard excess baggage

As we have already seen, the origins of low self-esteem can largely be traced to treatment we have received at the hands of others – excessively critical or overprotective parents, bullying peers, abusive relationships, life events that put us on the sidelines. But blaming those responsible, or wallowing in the garbage that has been dumped on us, doesn't take us far in addressing the problem. Too many people well into middle life are still raking over the damage caused by unjustified criticism or unrealistic parental expectation that took place 30 years previously. All the time you indulge in blaming or remain bound up in your status as victim, you are unlikely to make much progress in rectifying the damage. The perceived perpetrator is the one still in control of your feelings.

I'm afraid that in the blame-laying, compensation-seeking culture we inhabit these days, advising one's readers to forget about blame and to take on the responsibility for moving forward might seem to be an unfashionable thing to do. But if so, I'm happy to be unfashionable. On issues of self-esteem there really is no other option. Those who continue to harbour their sense of injury are destined to remain locked into the feelings of inferiority and humiliation.

I don't wish to downplay the enduring emotional hurt that may stem from the actions of others, or present you with one-size-fits-all pat solutions. I'm conscious that readers will have experienced very different levels of damaging behaviour and that for everyone, the degree of hurt is a very individual thing. But at the end of the day, you are the only person who can raise your self-esteem, and if there is a possibility that you might assist the process by relieving yourself of some excess baggage, then you should make every effort to do so. Obviously, the greater the perceived injury the harder it will be to leave it behind, and for some who have been on the receiving end of particularly abusive behaviour, it may be necessary to seek some professional assistance. Assuming that you feel ready and able to tackle your excess baggage, addressing the following 10 questions should help you to leave it behind:

1. *What excess baggage am I carrying that I would be better off without?* I'm not proposing that you turn this into a major exercise in self-examination, but give some consideration to those past injuries that are still niggling away at your self-esteem long after they should have ceased to have an effect. Jotting them down will probably help you to express them.

2. *What were the original injuries and how did I feel about them at the time?* Revisiting your feelings at the time may help you to get the issue into perspective. Would the bullying, criticism, humiliation, whatever, have had the same impact today? Was its effect greater then because you were more vulnerable in some way?

3. *In what ways might I have distorted or misinterpreted the original events?* As we have already seen, distortions and misinterpretations can play a major part in exaggerating our perceptions of injury. Be honest with yourself. Is there any way that you might have:
   - misinterpreted the motivation of the other person;
   - reached your conclusions on the basis of limited evidence;
   - overlooked contrary evidence;
   - exaggerated the importance of events?

4. *Am I using this baggage as a reason for self-pity?* This may not be comfortable to admit, but we often hang on to old indignities because they give us an excuse to feel sorry for ourselves. And we can use them to account for subsequent failures and missed aspirations. 'If it hadn't been for... I could have been...' – you know the sort of thing. Owning up to it means that you lose a source of blame, but it will help you to let go of the baggage and move on.

5. *Can I find any positive outcomes from the experiences?* You may not easily associate positive

outcomes with damaging and painful experiences, but surprisingly often there are things you can find. It may be that an instance of rejection led you in new and fulfilling directions or a failure took you into pastures new. Looking back from where you are now, it's possible that you will be able to see the positive outcomes that would not have been visible at the time the injury occurred. To take an example from my own experience: as a child and adolescent I was one of those weedy kids – always the last to be picked for the sports team – and suffered a considerable amount of bullying and abuse. For a long time I hung on to the humiliation of being the classroom wimp and harboured resentment towards those who had bullied me. But in my later teens I compensated by throwing myself into physical activity and transformed my level of fitness. The drive developed into a genuine lifelong love of sport and outdoor activity, so that today I should probably thank those bullies for providing the impetus for what is now one of the most satisfying features of my life.

6. *Do I need to share my sense of injury with somebody before I can leave it behind?* Sharing the issue with somebody else may help you to articulate it and to vent your feelings of grievance, but I hardly need to state that it needs to be the right person. Sounding off to an unsympathetic listener may do more harm than good. Almost as important as the person you choose is the timing. Don't just spring it on them. Let them know that you would like them to listen to something that has been seriously bugging you and pick a time when they will be able to give you their full attention.

7. *Do I need to address the perceived perpetrator in some way?* This may or may not be a good thing to

do. Raking up an issue long after the event may risk opening old wounds still further or it may help the process of healing. You will have to make a judgement. If you are in two minds about whether to confront the issue, it may help to obtain some impartial advice. Some people derive a deal of benefit from writing a letter that allows them to express their hurt, but that they subsequently do not send. This may be particularly effective if the offending individual is no longer around.

8. *How will it feel when I have rid myself of this baggage?* Concentrating on the sense of release you will have when you're free of this baggage will help to hasten the process of letting go.

9. *Can I genuinely forgive the perceived perpetrator?* If you can, it will greatly help you to move on. It may be that revisiting the issue allows you to see the perpetrator's actions in a more tolerant light – perhaps you can now see that, although they were mistaken, they were doing the best they knew in the circumstances. But don't get too hung up on forgiveness. If it's not there to give, you can't force it. More important that you put an end to the worm that has been eating at your self-esteem and, if necessary, forgive yourself – letting go of any residual guilt you have accumulated.

10. *How might I reward myself for letting go of this piece of excess baggage?* The idea of rewarding yourself might seem a little strange, but it helps to cement the process – reinforces the feel-good element. Letting go of excess baggage represents an achievement that deserves to be marked. So think of some treat or indulgence that will encourage you (not one that will make you feel guilty).

develop self-reliance

Excessive dependence on others is both a consequence of low self-esteem and an obstacle that prevents us from moving into more positive territory. Developing greater self-reliance allows us to experience the satisfaction that comes from meeting problems and challenges unaided and spares us negative, if often well-meaning, input from others. We demonstrate self-reliance when we:

- consult and listen to others but don't look to them to solve all our problems for us;
- express our views openly and honestly even though we know that others may not share them;
- follow a course of action we believe to be right in spite of negative comments from others;
- go about our business without constantly worrying about what others may think of us.

The first step towards achieving greater self-reliance is to observe yourself. Over-dependence on the opinions or support of others may have become a long-term habit you no longer notice. So take a few minutes to consider the following questions and jot down your answers.

Ask yourself:

- What occasions can I think of over the past three months when I wish I had shown greater independence of thought or action?
- What prevented me from doing so at the time?
- If I had been able to act with greater independence, what would the effect have been on my self-image?
- With the benefit of hindsight, were the obstacles that prevented me from acting more independently really as significant as they seemed at the time?

I suspect that one word that has most readily come to mind as you carry out this exercise is fear – fear of making a fool of yourself, fear of standing out against the crowd, fear of not being able to cope. And the problem with fears is that we so frequently allow them to assume an importance out of proportion with the scale of the challenge. More often than not, when we confront our fears, the reality turns out to be nowhere near as frightening as we had imagined it would be. We will look further into tackling your fears in Chapter 8, but in the meantime here are five steps to developing greater self-reliance:

1. *Look to your own resources first.* By all means seek help from others, but don't make it a knee-jerk response to any challenge. Needy individuals, whose first action is to lay their problems at the door of others, perpetuate their low self-esteem through a sense of dependence and inability to rise to challenges. They are also liable to invite patronising or even contemptuous responses on the part of others, which further undermine estimation of self. Before you seek out the assistance of others, aim to get a grip on the issues you are concerned with by asking yourself:
   – What exactly is the problem?
   – What courses of action are open to me?
   – Have I dealt with anything like this before?
   – What skills and knowledge of my own can I draw upon?
   – What resources or assistance might I need in order to resolve the problem?
   – Where might I most usefully look for some assistance?
   Tackling difficulties in this ordered way keeps you in control, allows you to approach others with clear, focused requests rather than general neediness. It prevents a scattergun approach to potential sources of help, liable to result in conflicting advice and assis-

tance. If you have been inclined to turn to others more frequently than necessary, you might be surprised to discover that some of your previous behaviour was simply habit, and that you have within you the resources to deal with many of the more difficult things that come your way.

2. *Don't strive to impress.* We all like to impress others, and there's nothing wrong with that. But there's a heap of difference between the effortless impressiveness that proceeds from strong self-belief and the needy boastfulness that is a characteristic of low self-esteem. Those who try too hard to impress crave the approval of others and, ironically, the harder they try the less satisfying the response they receive. I'm sure you can recall occasions when needy individuals have tried to impress you. The thoughts that come to you may be less than complimentary:

   - 'This needs to be taken with a pinch of salt.'
   - 'So what! Who does he think he's trying to impress?'
   - 'That guy is always boasting. It's a real bore talking to him.'
   - 'Is she trying to make me feel small or something?'

   By all means share your achievements with those who are able to find genuine and unconditional pleasure in your success. But for most of us, that will be a limited number of individuals. As for seeking to impress those within your wider sphere of acquaintance, let your actions and record do the talking. Unsolicited boasting reduces the value of an achievement. When you boast about an achievement you surrender ownership of it to others. Its value and significance to you is now to be measured by the response it receives and, beyond those who really care about you, people will seldom share the same sense of delight that you have in your achievements. So, every time you feel the need to boast or brag, you lose some of your inner strength and assurance. Far better for your self-esteem is the knowledge that you haven't needed to boast.

None of this means that you should hide your light under a bushel. Take all reasonable opportunities to demonstrate your capabilities and achievements, and recognise that there are occasions when structured boasting is the norm – in job interviews for example – but don't embark on a day-to-day process of talking yourself up to others just to keep feelings of inadequacy at bay.

Inner boasting is a different matter. You can do as much of that as you like and it will benefit your self-reliance. The benefits of affirmations and positive self-talk are covered at greater length in later chapters.

3. *Establish a self-reliance fitness programme.* Exercise is as important in building up self-reliance as it is in the development of physical strength and stamina. It's a matter of putting yourself in situations where your self-reliance is tested, proving to yourself that you can handle them and gradually building up the level of challenge in just the same way that you would with a physical training programme. It's important at every stage to set yourself a level of challenge that carries you a little further, but not so far that you will be completely daunted and lose confidence.

4. *Know your own mind.* Self-reliant people listen to the views of others, but have the independence of thought to make up their own minds and the courage not simply to run with the pack. They know where they are heading with clear goals and strategies for achieving them. Resolve that as part of your self-reliance fitness programme you will stand up more frequently for what you believe. You could surprise yourself.

5. *Maintain the right balance.* Self-reliance does not mean moving to the extremes of independence. You don't have to try to do everything for yourself. Such behaviour is often a perpetuation of low self-esteem. A healthy position is one where you are able to listen to the views of others but not to slavishly follow them if they don't accord with your own; and where you can ask others for help when you need it but not lean on them excessively.

So, before we leave this topic, just ask yourself whether there are examples of low self-esteem behaviour in your locker that are masquerading as self-reliance.

Ask yourself:

▧ Am I ever guilty of cutting myself off from others, ignoring wise counsel or stubbornly refusing all assistance?
▧ When does this tend to occur?
▧ In what situations can I establish a greater degree of balance between self-reliance and cooperation?

avoid unhealthy comparisons

There is no way that we can rid ourselves entirely of comparisons. They are thrust upon us in every aspect of our lives. You only have to open your Sunday newspaper to find yourself bombarded with lists of the country's top earners, last year's smart investments, this year's top style tips and next year's house price hotspots. It's a sturdy soul who can get through that lot without feeling they have fallen short in some way.

You can make an argument for the value of comparisons of course. When they're positive they make us feel good. Who doesn't get a lift from knowing that they got the highest marks in the group, or that they've beaten the competition to a promotion, a contract or the next round of a sporting event? But there's a point at which comparisons cease to be healthy. It comes when you can only feel good about yourself by comparing yourself with someone in a worse position, or when you punish yourself by finding constant reasons to compare yourself unfavourably against other people or against some idealised model of what you feel you should be achieving.

Give yourself an unhealthy-comparisons check:
Within recent weeks have you:

- ▓ compared yourself unfavourably with somebody else who appears to have more style, poise, confidence, general attractiveness;
- ▓ chastised yourself for not achieving as much as a colleague, friend or relative;
- ▓ worried that you are earning less than some other people no more deserving than you;
- ▓ envied another's skills or possessions;
- ▓ felt the need to seek out other people's shortcomings in order to bolster yourself?

Every time you engage in this sort of comparative activity, you present your negative self-image with plenty of ammunition. And once you get into the habit of making comparisons, you will always find somebody who appears to be doing better than you.

Comparisons often focus on just one aspect of an individual's life, but we use them to draw wholly unsupportable conclusions. We may, for example, assume that because somebody else has achieved more career success than we have, they must as a consequence be happier and more fulfilled than we are in all other features of their life. This is another example of the distorted thinking we engage in that selects the most negative features of our own experience and sets it alongside the most positive features of somebody else's.

And what of the millstones that comparisons hang around our necks? As soon as you start to compare yourself unfavourably, you introduce a set of *shoulds* into your life:

- ▨ I should have a car like that.
- ▨ I should be doing at least as well.
- ▨ I should try to look like that.

They are a further instance of handing control of your life and happiness to others. Goals and aspirations are valuable things to have – they can boost your self-esteem and help you to approach challenges with confidence. But they must be your own goals, formulated on the basis of the things that really matter to your own fulfilment, not a set of wants that are simply culled from a negative sense that others are outdoing you.

So, set out your stall and be sure that it is truly yours. When measuring how well you are doing, try to make the comparison with your own progress over time rather than always looking to see whether you are one up on others. Be on the lookout for any tendency to reach for comparisons. You may find that it has become almost an unconscious habit. Pounce on them and ask yourself, 'How does this comparison benefit my self-esteem?' Steer clear of those whose conversation habitually leads to unhealthy comparisons – boastful individuals who always seek to talk up their acquisitions and achievements. Generally they are rather needy people who are in the game of boosting their own self-esteem.

3

value yourself

While the initial causes of low self-esteem might lie with negative life events and the behaviour of others towards us, much of what keeps it going is our own failure to value ourselves and to pay due note to our talents and achievements. We ignore our good qualities, constantly criticise our own performance, punish ourselves for the most minor of errors and set ourselves impossible standards. This chapter is about starting to make a change and treating ourselves with more respect.

recognise your qualities

It's very common to overlook one's good qualities and concentrate solely on the bad. So, I'd like you now to do a little digging into the positive aspects of yourself. To set your thought processes whirring, here is a list of 65 adjectives. Identify the ones you think may apply to you and add others that occur to you as you go through the list. If you're inclined to self-deprecation, you may find yourself hesitating over some items. So be sure to give yourself the benefit of the doubt on any qualities about which you feel uncertain.

Adventurous
Astute
Attentive
Calm
Carefree
Careful
Charming
Clear-sighted
Committed
Communicative
Considerate
Courageous
Courteous
Creative
Curious
Diplomatic
Direct
Discerning
Easy-going
Encouraging
Enigmatic
Flexible
Forceful
Friendly
Fun-loving
Generous
Gentle
Hard-working
Honest
Humorous
Individualistic
Influential

Ingenious
Inspirational
Intelligent
Interested
Kind-hearted
Loyal
Methodical
Observant
Optimistic
Organised
Persuasive
Pragmatic
Principled
Reasonable
Relaxed
Reliable
Responsible
Self-motivated
Single-minded
Skilled
Sociable
Stoical
Straightforward
Strong-willed
Sympathetic
Tactful
Thoughtful
Tough when necessary
Uncomplicated
Understanding
Versatile
Vigilant
Wise

I defy you to complete this exercise and be able to say at the end of it that you have nothing going for you. You have many positive qualities. It's just that in the hurly-burly of life there is a tendency to lose sight of them or take them for granted. Hang on to the positive qualities you have recognised and be sure to give yourself credit for them.

---

save it for later

As you worked through this exercise, you may have identified qualities that would benefit your self-esteem, but which you do not currently possess or are less prominent than you would wish. Make a note of them. I would like to return to them in the next chapter when we look at developing new beliefs.

---

acknowledge your achievements

Achievements represent solid ground from which you can build your self-esteem. They offer a foothold on those occasions when self-doubt starts to creep over you, and provide you with powerful evidence to support a new more positive view of yourself. So it's well worth spending some time reflecting upon them. Producing an achievement list is a good way to do this. Putting your achievements down on paper is a lot more meaningful than just thinking about them. It gives you a reference you can return to and update. If you are customarily self-deprecating, you are unlikely at first to find this the most comfortable task in the world. The list seems so thin to start with. Many people struggle to find more than a handful of things they consider achievements, and regard even the ones they identify as pretty pathetic. Part of this is down to natural reluctance to blow your own trumpet, but it's also about the way we characterise achievements. We tend to think only of those that have been marked by some form of public recognition – qualification milestones, job promotions, awards. But the achievements that matter most in terms of our self-belief are often those that may be known only to ourselves.

It is an achievement:

- ▦ every time you face up to fear;
- ▦ every time you confront a problem;
- ▦ every time you handle a difficult situation;
- ▦ every time you bounce back from a disappointment.

We often misperceive such occasions as failures because they are associated with some discomfort, and we tend to remember just the bad things about the situation – the anxiety, fear or disappointment. So dig out those real achievements, large and small. And don't feel self-conscious about writing them down; there's nobody looking over your shoulder. If it feels unduly self-congratulatory and you're inclined to downplay some of your accomplishments, give yourself the best friend treatment. Imagine that the achievements are not yours but those of a good friend, and ask yourself how you would regard them if you were talking to that person.

It's one of the unfortunate features of memory that one painful experience may stick with us far longer than a string of moderate successes. So use a diary to record new achievements as they occur and before they slip away. As you become more accustomed to recording your accomplishments it will feel easier and more natural.

There is a positive spillover between achievements in different aspects of our lives. So, whatever the achievements – facing up to your fear of heights on a climbing wall, handling a tricky family problem – put them down. If they are meaningful to you, they will make a difference. Using the following headings may help to jog your memory about achievements in different areas of your life:

- ▦ home and family;
- ▦ education;
- ▦ work;
- ▦ leisure and personal development;
- ▦ contribution and community.

stifle internal criticism

Who is your greatest critic? Is there anybody who gives you a harder time than yourself? Do you set yourself standards that you would regard as wholly unreasonable if anyone else were to expect them of you? When you fail to measure up, do you subject yourself to strictures you wouldn't dream of imposing on others – rage, guilt and self-condemnation?

If you found yourself answering 'Yes' to any of the above questions, think about giving yourself a break and treating yourself with greater respect. Scolding and abuse are seldom the way to get the best out of people, and this applies whether somebody else is berating you or you are berating yourself.

I'm not suggesting here that you cease to set targets – they can be an important factor in boosting self-esteem. Nor am I proposing that you make your standards less than demanding. Only that you take care not to make them unreasonable or impossible, and that on those occasions when you fall a little short of what you had hoped to achieve, you don't treat it as evidence of your worthlessness and an occasion for punishment rather than recovery.

Even if you are not yet at the point of putting the thumbscrews on yourself, you may still be engaging in far more self-criticism than is good for you. Much of the damage is done by regular low-level self-deprecation and negative self-talk. There are a number of things you can do to change the way you work with yourself.

ask yourself some questions

Questioning yourself is an excellent way to expose irrationality, exaggeration and double standards in your attitude towards your thoughts and actions. When you feel inclined to criticise yourself, stop and ask:

■ Is this mistake really as important as I am making out? What are the probable consequences of it?

■ Am I just concentrating on the negative things here? What can I pull out of this that is positive?

■ Am I placing expectations on myself that are unreasonable?

■ Just because I feel foolish at this moment, does that make me into a fool?

■ Why am I so bothered about this? Is it because I am frightened of what other people will think of me?

■ Am I leaping to conclusions about what others will think? And even if they do think badly of me, does it really matter?

reprogram your self-talk

For years you may have been engaging in a routine negative internal dialogue with yourself that is so commonplace that you have ceased to notice it. We all do it at some time – slagging ourselves off whenever we make mistakes, calling ourselves idiots over minor errors and omissions, or cursing our stupidity when faced with oversights and memory lapses. It may seem like harmless stuff – just a low-level running commentary on our performance – but cumulatively it can be damaging. This internal dialogue is likely to be deeply ingrained, and all negative self-talk definitely has a detrimental effect on resolve and self-esteem. There are no plus points to it.

Through long habit we have programmed ourselves to react in this way, and to change our behaviour we need some conscious reprogramming. So keep your internal ears tuned for those occasions when you might be tempted quietly to berate yourself and take steps to substitute positive statements – affirmations – for the negative ones you would normally utter. Instead of saying to yourself, 'You idiot, what did you have to do that for?' say something like, 'This is a setback I can easily overcome.' It's a technique that will feel unnatural, even foolish, at first, but persist and you should be able to seriously reduce the number of negative messages you feed yourself.

When choosing affirmations, select strong positive statements in the first person. 'I can choose the way I respond' is a better example of a positive affirmation than 'Other people don't influence my responses.' Your affirmations should be vigorous and punchy but not silly or incredible. You won't believe them if they are. So, 'I am the champion of the world' is probably not a good idea. Get yourself a stock of affirmations that you can repeat regularly to yourself, not just when you are under pressure, but at other quiet times – when you are driving to and from work for example, or at the beginning and end of your day. It's important that you choose statements that are meaningful to you, not just off-the-peg examples, but to get you started, here are one or two ideas:

- ▦ I believe in my ability to succeed.
- ▦ I am calm and in control.
- ▦ I can find a solution to every problem.
- ▦ I enjoy meeting challenges.

dispel outward self-criticism

'Oh, don't ask me to do it. I'm bound to get it wrong.'
'Of course, me being me, it was a complete disaster.'
'Here's the report you asked for. I'm afraid it isn't very good.'

Putting yourself down in front of others can be even more damaging than the internal dialogue you have with yourself. You still send 'worthlessness' messages to yourself but you send them to others too. Moderate self-deprecation linked to humour can be an attractive trait that offers benefits for both the speaker and the listener, but the persistent belittling of oneself has no redeeming features. People may correct you – 'I'm sure it's excellent work as usual' – but some of the negative messages you are presenting about yourself will rub off. Those who constantly present themselves as losers will come to be regarded as such, at least by some. It may be that your habit of putting yourself down arises from uncertainty about how others will receive your efforts or embarrassment about blowing your own trumpet. You may be getting in first as a way of forestalling any criticism that is in the offing. Whatever the source of the behaviour, try to curb it. Break the habit by substituting neutral or positive statements.

be more of a friend to yourself

What are your expectations of friends? Do you expect them never to make mistakes, never to show weakness, never to make fools of themselves? Of course not. You accept them as human beings with all their flaws and failings and, out of the fondness and respect you have for them, you forgive their lapses and transgressions. OK, if you can do it for a friend, why can't you do it for yourself? The answer is that you can, but once again it's a matter of breaking the habit of years. So when you're knocking yourself, just remember that it's your best friend you're insulting – this person deserves a bit more of your respect.

laugh

Suggesting that you laugh at yourself might seem directly to contradict my earlier point about changing your internal dialogue, but I don't believe it has to be so. There is a distinction to be made between laughing at yourself and some of the more destructive forms of self-deprecation. Laughing at yourself does not have to be about putting yourself down. To seek out the humour in your own actions means knowing yourself to a degree, recognising and accepting your human frailties and shortcomings. In other words, you need to like yourself and be interested in what makes you tick. So don't take yourself too seriously. Observe yourself as you would a lovable but slightly eccentric friend, and it will benefit your self-esteem.

Laughter is also a wonderful stress buster, an essential skill of the survivor. Searching out the humour in your situation allows you to step back and get it in perspective with none of the self-condemnation that so frequently accompanies occasions when we find ourselves under pressure. And be sure to laugh at the time it will do you the most good – when the pain and discomfort is still fresh. That way you will boost your resilience and bounce back from failures and disappointments more rapidly.

Try it. Take an example of an occasion when you criticised and punished yourself, and retell it to yourself with humour. It feels a lot better, doesn't it?

accept praise

How do you react when somebody offers you praise on a job well done or compliments your appearance, your cooking or your taste? Do you accept the plaudits with grace and appreciation or throw them back at the giver?

'Oh this old thing! It's just something I bought in a sale.'
'I didn't think it was much cop. The meat was underdone and the vegetables were ruined.'
'I'm sure you're trying to be kind, but really…'
'Are you making some kind of a joke?'

Difficulty in accepting praise is a very common form of self-deprecation indicative of low self-esteem. It's ironic that at one and the same time you can be heavily dependent on the approval of others and yet unable to deal with it when it is expressed. Don't pretend to yourself that this kind of behaviour is simply old-fashioned modesty. When you turn down or deflect a compliment you are telling yourself and the compliment-giver that you are unworthy of it and you are damning yourself as much as when you criticise or put yourself down. And it's true that when an individual repeatedly throws back praise, others are inclined to stop offering it. So, if you're prone to this sort of behaviour, stop it. Accept praise that comes your way and take pleasure in it. And give praise too whenever you see it is deserved; you'll find even more comes your way. As with everything there is a balance to be struck. Don't go to the other end of the praise spectrum where you are fishing for compliments or dishing out unwarranted plaudits in the hope of an equally meaningless return. That displays a neediness that is equally indicative of low self-esteem. Of course, it has to be recognised that some praise is insincerely given, is patronising or is wildly over the top. In such circumstances a little humour and gentle self-deprecation may be in order, but this is a far cry from routinely refusing to accept praise.

avoid double jeopardy

Silencing the internal critic isn't just a matter of paying attention to the internal and external dialogue we use in respect of our immediate actions. More damaging by far can be the effect of constant critical raking over of the past. How often do you:

■ revisit the mistakes you have made and curse your stupidity;
■ relive the pain and shame of social blunders and faux pas;
■ castigate yourself for past decisions that have turned out to be less than successful?

This self-punishment can become something of an obsession. You spend far too much time analysing events long past, endlessly going over the options you had and the actions you should have taken. And each time you engage in such behaviour, you deliver further blows to your self-esteem. If you are inclined to this sort of activity, it can be difficult to cure yourself, but it's important that you make the effort. Here are five steps to making a difference:

1. Recognise that there is a place for analysis of past actions, but its purpose is to help you develop, to give you insights that will assist you in being more effective, not to batter yourself into the ground. So ask yourself questions that take you forward. Instead of saying, 'How could I be so stupid?', ask yourself, 'What might I do differently in the future?' or 'What positive lessons can I take from this experience?'

2. Impose a time limit that is appropriate to the issue in question. There is a sell-by date after which further analysis moves into negative territory. I can't be specific about its length; with some major life setbacks you may need time to get over the shock and the pain before you can look at lessons with any degree of rationality. But you will know you have gone beyond it when you find yourself repeatedly going over the same ground, causing yourself renewed pain, but gaining no new insights. Use positive affirmations to help you move on.

3. Accept that you will never get it entirely right. Expecting to do so suggests a tendency towards perfectionism. All the time you spend dwelling on past imperfections is time you could be more profitably using to improve your present performance. So, by drawing a line under your errors you are making it less likely that you will look back on today with regret.

4. Regain your sense of proportion. That faux pas you keep revisiting still makes you blush with shame, but was it really as dreadful as your memory makes it out to be? Chances are that you are guilty of some mental exaggeration over time. And what of the people who witnessed it – the real reason for your embarrassment

– do they still have any recollection of your blunder? Try this little exercise:

- Spend two or three minutes jotting down all the recollections you can bring to mind of blunders you have committed that still make you cringe.
- Now spend the same amount of time listing similar blunders you can recall being committed by others.
- Compare your lists.

I'm willing to bet that your own cringe situations came much more readily to mind than those of other people. And I would hazard a guess that those on the second list are primarily stories others have told you to highlight their own embarrassment or situations where your overriding emotion was not ridicule but sympathy towards the individual concerned.

5. Beware of sitting in judgement with the benefit of hindsight. It's easy looking back on events and decisions to see better alternative courses of action. New information may well have emerged that, had you known it then, might have resulted in a better decision. You may have gained new insights and skills since, or even from, the event. The only meaningful judgement you can make of your actions is in relation to the skills and information you were able to call upon at the time.

Owning up to ourselves that we have blundered has a value. The pain and discomfort we experience can provide the best possible leverage for changing our behaviour in the future. But too much pain will push us in the direction of safety. We will be too scared to emerge from the comfort zone and repeat the experience and so will shrink from what we perceive as similar situations. So, accept the pain of a bad decision or a foolish action for just long enough to build up a head of steam for change and then move on. And make sure that any judgement is confined solely to your actions and not to your basic human worth. We all make bad decisions, mistakes and errors. They do not make us into worthless individuals.

exercise

Before leaving this section, just give a little thought to setting an agenda for dumping those events that are past their sell-by date:

- ▓ What are the events it is time to release yourself from?
- ▓ In what way might you have exaggerated any of them out of proportion to the original error or embarrassment?
- ▓ What further positive lessons can you extract from them?
- ▓ How can you ensure that they will do you no further damage?

tackle perfectionism

What's wrong with being a perfectionist? It's a trait that people are often prepared to own up to, after all. The comment, 'I'm a bit of perfectionist' is more often uttered with a smile than an apology. And perfectionists are frequently very successful individuals. So is there really a place for a section on perfectionism in a book about raising self-esteem? Well yes there is. Perfectionism is a manifestation of low self-esteem and can be a serious handicap to one's fulfilment and enjoyment of life.

are you a perfectionist?

Look at the following 10 statements and answer yes or no to each:

- ▓ I avoid things if I think that I won't be able to do them well.

■ I feel let down by other people in my life – partner, colleagues, friends, children.

■ I become angry with myself if ever I make a mistake.

■ I would sooner do a task myself than delegate it.

■ Even when I receive praise for a job well done, I still feel dissatisfied with my performance.

■ People call me a control freak or a nit-picker.

■ I hate the idea of being just average.

■ I feel that if I don't do well, people may reject me.

■ I get annoyed with myself because I'm unable to tackle all the things I want to do.

■ I feel that one flaw in an otherwise good piece of work can ruin the whole thing.

If you have found yourself answering yes to any of these, then you may have a tendency towards perfectionism. Perfectionism can express itself in different ways. It may be seen in the excessive demands you make of yourself, the high expectations you have of others or the feeling that other people and society in general has high expectations of you. And it can embrace any aspect of our lives – achievement at work, pursuit of physical perfection, seeking after an ideal relationship, or an obsessive tendency towards neatness and organisation in our lives. All of it is behaviour that arises from low self-esteem and displays the following characteristics:

■ a sense that only by being perfect can you feel truly worthwhile;

■ difficulty in accepting criticism or acknowledging mistakes;

■ very limited satisfaction from achievements.

Perfectionists are motivated more by the fear of failure than the prospect of success. They are desperate to succeed but petrified of failing. This may lead them to be risk averse – remaining in the comfort zone and avoiding challenges, or procrastinating rather than getting started on a task that may not lead to complete success. They are also inclined to give up on a task that is progressing less than perfectly. They may set themselves particularly low targets that can be met with ease or, conversely, set impossibly high targets that they have no hope of achieving. Neither strategy lends itself to the fulfilment of potential.

Perfectionists are seldom content with their current situation because there are always aspects of it that fall short of their expectations. While there might be some pluses to be had from the high standards we perfectionists set ourselves (yes, I will admit to some of it) they are outweighed by the minuses that come in the form of self-imposed stress, anger and frustration as we constantly run up against ideals we cannot achieve.

'But,' you may say, 'setting my sights high is one of the things that bolsters my self-esteem. And it's one of the messages coming out of this book. Why else would you include a chapter on setting and achieving goals?'

Sure! But striving after an unrealistic standard that you fail to achieve and that makes you miserable is no way to go. You can still set your sights high and seek after excellence in what you do while removing some of the negative aspects of perfectionism. Here are six ways to set about it.

overcoming perfectionism

1. The first step to beating perfectionism is to recognise the tendency in yourself. Jot down the things you do in the various parts of your life that demonstrate unrealistically high expectations of yourself or others. If you have difficulty doing this, you may find it useful to enlist the help of your partner, a close friend or colleague. Don't be defensive about it. Approach the task in a spirit of readiness to accept some shortcomings – they are what help to make us human. And

if you find it uncomfortable, balance the exercise by revisiting the one on positive qualities at the beginning of this chapter.

2. Be clear about what you are missing. It's a good idea to write down all the ways you can think of in which perfectionist behaviour handicaps you. This helps rid you of the stubborn notion that somehow a perfectionist is quite a good thing to be. Retain the list and refer to it at times when you find yourself slipping back into old ways.

3. Settle for good in some things when you would normally seek exceptional. This doesn't mean going for sub-standard, simply recognising that you cannot expect to deliver perfection all the time, and that the extra stress and effort involved in constantly striving for the absolute pinnacle often outweighs the benefits. Set deadlines for those tasks that you tend to treat in a perfectionist manner and resolve that you will not work on them beyond that time, whether or not they meet your normal exacting standards. Experience the extra energy and enjoyment that comes when you take the pressure off yourself. Be more ready to target those things where you will give your utmost and those where you will be content simply to be good.

4. Give yourself permission to fail on occasions. Recognise the way in which your thinking can become distorted by the fear of failure. Remember that failure is seldom as catastrophic as your fearful imaginings paint it to be and it seldom results in you being liked or respected less. In fact, if you deal well with failure you may greatly enhance others' opinions of you. What's more, failure can be an enlightening and energising experience. It can spark new awareness and give you the opportunity to rethink your approach to challenges. The person who is able to use failure constructively can move on to greater levels of success.

5. Talk to others. If you feel that you have to be perfect in order to gain the approval of those who matter to you, talk to a trusted friend about it. This may not be easy to do, but the benefits could be considerable. Admitting our shortcomings rather than seeking to bottle them up can offer a great sense of relief and will generally produce a positive response from those who have our interests at heart. You will find that perfection isn't the quality that makes people likeable or lovable; rather it is our weaknesses, those things that make us human. If the sort of conversation I have described is a daunting prospect for you, then just consider how you would respond if a good friend approached you with their fears and concerns. Would you like them any less? Would you belittle them? I think not. I suggest you would be pleased that they had chosen to share this problem with you and more than happy for the chance to help.

6. Get into other people's shoes. If an aspect of your perfectionism is a lack of realism in your expectations of others, or feedback has led you to believe that you have a tendency to be too controlling, make a deliberate and concerted effort to see life from other people's perspective. Expecting others always to conform to your view of the world is as debilitating for you as it is for them. You waste precious energy on a quest that is as pointless as trying to herd cats. Accepting other people's standards on occasions does not have to mean that yours are consigned to the bin. It's just part of the give and take that allows us all to rub along in this world. Clinging to your standards and ways of doing things may feel like an essential part of your self-esteem, but in fact it is an expression of your feelings of inadequacy. Loosen up. Why should your way be the only one to count?

There is clearly a line to be drawn between the positive quest for excellence (good for self-esteem) and perfectionism (bad for self-esteem). You might be asking yourself quite where it falls and how to ensure that you remain on the right side of it. I would suggest that staying on the healthy side of the line is largely a matter of maintaining balance in your life. You should suspect that you have stepped over it if:

▨ your pursuit of excellence leaves you unable to derive any pleasure from activities;

▨ you can only discover a sense of fulfilment when an activity you are engaged in is without any flaws whatsoever;

▨ the driving force behind your quest for excellence is the need to prove yourself to others, to impress or to be accepted by them.

It may be difficult for you to accept that the standards you are expecting of yourself or others are too high. They quite possibly feel like the absolute minimum to maintain dignity and self-respect. But the problem may not be to do with the absolute standards you are seeking so much as standards that are relative to the current situation and reasonable given the timescale and resources you are working with. So it's OK to be striving for a very high goal providing that you are working to a realistic action plan that takes account of the base from which you are starting, your current level of skills and the other demands that there are upon you.

seek out positive people

Just as your self-esteem may be damaged by the drip-feed of self-generated negative messages, so too it can suffer if you are all the time in the company of negative-minded people. I'm not talking here about those who are out to damage you; I'm referring to members of the 'ain't it awful' brigade – people who seem compelled to look for the downside in any situation. They may present themselves as caring and supportive friends or colleagues, but their 'support' frequently consists of encouragement to wallow with them in their own brand of negativity and whingeing about others. All of us are affected by those with whom we spend our daily lives, and if you are surrounded by constant negativity it can seriously undermine any attempts you may be making in the direction of more positive thinking. So seek the company, whenever you can, of those whose positive vibes are going to boost you and your view of your own capabilities.

Of course, not all your regular associates are likely to be of your own choosing. It may be that you have been placed in a negatively minded work group. In such a situation you have three options: put up with it, seek to change it or get out. Getting out may be economically unfeasible, and putting up with it may seem the easiest thing to do. You can build yourself a shell, limit your interaction and get on with your job. However, it's hard to isolate yourself completely from a negative atmosphere, and it may seem like a lonely furrow to plough.

But it is possible to exert a positive influence. Don't assume that a team climate that is predominantly negative enjoys the support of everyone in it. Generally it is determined by one or two dominant individuals and there will be others who are going for an easy life, keeping their heads down, but who could be turned around to a more positive way of thinking and behaving. Such people won't publicise their presence as markedly as the whingers, but if you keep your eyes and ears open you can start to locate them and to build constructive relationships. With the support of two or three you may be able to inject a more positive tone, which will carry still more members of the group with you.

You can be an architect for change. It is within your power to select your own attitude. Resolve that you will not have it determined by others, and refuse to go along with the gloom. Make a deliberate attempt to seek out the humour and enjoyment in your day-to-day activities, and make others aware of your appreciation of any actions they take that lift the mood. It may surprise you how influential you can be.

take charge of your beliefs

What beliefs do you hold about yourself and the way you live your life? It's a pretty broad question and you might find yourself initially stumped for an answer. But bear with me. I am not thinking here about grand cosmic beliefs or religious convictions, but about the scores, hundreds maybe, of taken-for-granted beliefs that lie behind your day-to-day actions – beliefs about yourself, beliefs about others, beliefs about the way the world works. Here are some examples of the sort of thing I mean:

- I am a lucky/unlucky person (belief about self).
- If you show that you trust people, they will generally respond positively (belief about others).
- There's no such thing as a free lunch (belief about the way the world works).

exercise

Take a blank sheet of paper and spend a few minutes jotting down all the beliefs you can think of that you apply as you go about your life.

You may find it initially a little difficult to get started, but stick with it until you have at least 12 to 15 examples on paper. This will only be a small proportion of the beliefs that guide your life, but at this stage I just want to use them for illustrative purposes.

Some of the things you have jotted down may have quite a minor effect on the way you conduct your life, whereas others are absolutely fundamental. But all will have some impact because what you believe will determine how you act. Our lives are shaped not so much by events, as by our responses to those events, and the way we respond will be largely down to our beliefs. For example, if it is your belief that people will generally react positively when they are trusted, then you are going to behave more openly towards others than somebody who believes that the world is out to rip them off. In all sorts of ways your daily actions will give flesh to that belief. If you believe you are a lucky person, you are less likely to shrink from a risky challenge than those who believe themselves to be unlucky. So, as a 'lucky' person you more frequently put yourself in a position where your 'luck' can be shown to have paid off

enabling and limiting beliefs

Take another look at the things you have jotted down in the exercise above. You will notice that some of them lead you in a positive direction, helping you to unlock your potential and become the sort of person you want to be – we might call them enabling beliefs. Others hold you back and prevent you from living a full and enjoyable life – we might call these limiting beliefs.

Enabling

- There is always something useful to be learned from even the worst experiences.
- Fortune favours the brave.
- I'm as worthwhile as anyone else on the planet.

Limiting

- There is no point in trying to change the way you are.
- People like me always get the bad breaks.
- You can't teach an old dog new tricks.

exercise

Go through your list separating the beliefs you have identified according to whether they are enabling or limiting. Please don't be tempted to skip this task – it's important. You don't need to write the items out again, just mark them with a tick or a cross to indicate enabling or limiting. Now give some thought to the relative importance of the identified items. Some of the points you have jotted down will have much greater impact on your attitude and your behaviour than others. Have a go at arranging, in order of their importance, the beliefs that most enable you and those that most limit you.

So where did these beliefs that can have such an impact on our thinking and behaviour come from? There is a tendency for us to regard them as fixed and immutable. We can't recall a time when we didn't hold them, and it's easy to conclude that they are simply a part of the way we are. In fact they have been built up in a piecemeal fashion as a result of our experiences and the influence of others upon us. There's nothing sacrosanct about them at all – some may have been constructed on the flimsiest of foundations. Perhaps some of yours were:

- ▓ adopted at a time when your maturity and experience of life was much less than it is now;
- ▓ developed as a consequence of one or two incidents that are unrepresentative of your general experience;
- ▓ founded on misinterpretations of your own or other people's behaviour;
- ▓ adopted as cover for feelings of failure and inadequacy.

People who lack self-belief are liable to have a disproportionate number of limiting beliefs that lack validity but may fuel a pattern of behaviour resulting in a vicious circle of low self-esteem:

Vicious circle of low self-esteem

1. I am not an attractive person (limiting belief).
2. If I approach those I find attractive I will suffer painful rejection.
3. I will only respond if the people I find attractive approach me.
4. The fact that the people I find attractive are not approaching me confirms that I am not an attractive person.

The effect of some beliefs, individually or in concert, may be enough to put us into a state of acquired helplessness. Let's consider the example of a person I shall call Jenny. She has a collection of limiting beliefs, three of which are as follows:

- ▓ Other people are generally brighter and more competent than me.
- ▓ I can never stick at anything for long enough to see it through.
- ▓ Other people always take advantage of me.

Other people are generally brighter and more competent than me. This belief was acquired in childhood and adolescence when comparisons were made at school and in the home with Jenny's high-flying sisters. She now routinely underrates her abilities, discounting clear evidence that she is of above average intelligence and has many skills. And she so routinely lets others know her poor opinion of her own abilities that some of them take her at her word.

I can never stick at anything for long enough to see it through. Jenny has generalised from a couple of examples to construct what has become a self-fulfilling prophecy and either enters any new challenge with an attitude already resigned to the prospect of failure or, for the same reason, bottles out on challenges altogether.

Other people always take advantage of me. If Jenny persists in this belief she will continue to approach situations in a frame of mind where she expects to be taken advantage of. Her antennae will be highly tuned to pick up signals that suggest she is being taken for granted, overlooked, ripped off, done down. Not all of these will be accurate interpretations and, of those that are, some of the behaviour she experiences may arise from the very victim-type attitude she is presenting to others.

changing your beliefs

You really can change your beliefs. And not just the ones that have arisen from distortions and exaggerations, even those limiting beliefs that may seem to have firm foundations are not set in stone. You are the one who developed them and gave them their importance as rules for living, and you can change them.

So it's time to set about giving your beliefs a thorough examination – distinguishing between those you want to retain as a part of your future and those that you would be better off discarding.

exercise

The exercise you did earlier to identify your limiting and enabling beliefs was a valuable one, but will only take you so far. There are doubtless many more influences upon you than you were able to think about in the few minutes you gave to the task. So I would like you to put yourself under observation for the next two or three weeks and catch any instances of beliefs that you would want to dispel or reinforce. The best way to do this is to note down those things you would like to remove or strengthen at the time they occur to you. If you routinely carry a notebook, organiser or diary with you, head up two blank pages as follows: 'Things I want to stop thinking' and 'Things I want to start believing'. Alternatively, head up a pair of blank postcards in the same way and carry them with you. Whenever you find yourself being held back by a limiting belief, or the possibility of a new, positive way of thinking occurs to you, note it down.

discarding limiting and redundant beliefs

You may recognise a belief as limiting but it can still be very difficult to let it go. It may have become part of the way you see yourself or you may be using it as an excuse for inaction. So the first step is to recognise it for what it is – a piece of learned behaviour that is holding you back You have left all manner of beliefs behind as you have gone through life. Do you really hold the identical beliefs you held as a child and an adolescent? Of course you don't. Know then that it is possible and make the decision that obsolete and unhelpful beliefs will no longer feature in your repertoire. Next, get to grips with the belief by asking yourself some questions:

- ▓ How did this belief come about?
- ▓ Are there other beliefs underlying it?
- ▓ Does it have any real basis in fact?
- ▓ What have been the effects of it? How is it damaging me?
- ▓ Why have I hung on to it for so long? What are the costs of me abiding by it?

Questioning will frequently help you to uncover fundamental flaws in the thinking that has led to your negative and limiting beliefs. It gives you the ammunition with which to attack them and makes you painfully aware of the damage they are doing to you. The negative belief is exposed as an intruder rather than a cosy element of your natural make-up.

When Jenny questions her belief that she is unable to stick at anything long enough to see it through, she realises that it dates back to the time when she dropped out of university after a lengthy bout of glandular fever and a failed relationship. She has been handicapping herself for 10 years as a result of one incident that, although highly significant at the time, was totally understandable in the circumstances.

search out contrary evidence

Your beliefs may have been founded on flimsy evidence. You may have drawn conclusions from just one or two instances or misinterpreted situations altogether. But even when your beliefs appear to have firm foundations, you are bound to have been in some way selective in the evidence you have used to support the view you have come to. There is always contrary evidence – evidence that discounts the negative view you have arrived at. It is just as legitimate as any you have used to come to your original conclusions. So seek it out and use it to dismiss the limiting beliefs and support more positive enabling beliefs.

tackle small foes as well as large

Don't just go for the major, well-embedded beliefs. Tackle some of the more easy targets too. Success in this quarter will give you a sense of progress and the conviction that you can shift larger impediments.

remove negative self-talk

Negative self-talk nourishes limiting beliefs. I'm referring to those occasions when you are under pressure and the belief is articulated in your mind – 'These people are brighter than me. I'm bound to get it wrong and make a fool of myself.' Keep your internal ears open for examples of negative self-talk and stamp on it firmly.

recast the belief

Ditching a negative belief is more difficult if you have nothing to put in its place, so work on the positive statements that you aim to be guided by in future. It may be possible to look at the original negative belief in a slightly different way – to recast it so that it becomes a positive rather than a negative influence on the way you conduct your life. You can often find some gems of positive thinking to work upon in the most negative of beliefs.

change the landscape in which the belief flourishes

Expecting to remove a limiting belief while all the conditions that nurtured it remain unchanged is asking a lot of yourself. So search out those things that nourish the belief and seek to isolate or remove them. If the source of nourishment is the influence of other people, it may be necessary to scale down the level of interaction with those individuals. If the source is long-standing habit on your part you may need to embark on a habit-busting blitz to decisively shift your patterns of behaviour. Let's say, for example, that you believe there is never any time to tackle the things that are important to you. Perhaps this belief is able to flourish because of poor time management and personal organisation. Tackling these problems through a sustained attack on your work habits may be what is needed to shift the belief.

developing new positive beliefs

Just as you can unlearn the negative beliefs that have been holding you back, so it is possible to take on new beliefs that will empower you and boost your self-esteem. The process is not too different from the way you picked up all your current beliefs, but whereas they were acquired mainly in a random hotchpotch of responses to experiences, your new beliefs will be targeted and actively promoted. If that seems like a case of manipulating your own thoughts, then I make no apology for it. There is nobody with more right to manipulate your thoughts than you, and you have been doing it unconsciously for years anyway. Here are the steps towards developing new enabling beliefs:

1. *Identify desirable qualities.* Remember the exercise in the previous chapter in which you identified your positive qualities? I suggested at the time that you make a note of any additional qualities you would like to develop and which would aid your self-esteem. Now is the time to dig out that note. If you had difficulty identifying additional desirable qualities, think about the people you most admire and the qualities they display.

2. *Match them to beliefs and behaviour.* Now consider what beliefs about yourself you will need if you are going to develop these desirable qualities. Let's assume that a quality you want to develop is calmness, you might articulate the necessary belief as: 'I believe I can deal with anything life throws at me without panicking.'

   What sort of behaviour would you expect from people who held those beliefs? You might think about coping coolly with a workplace crisis, dealing with a home emergency, resolving a problem on holiday. Situations could involve pacifying others who are angry or upset, or taking the pressure without getting upset yourself.

3. *Find examples.* What examples can you find of yourself behaving in this way? If you dig around, you may be surprised to discover evidence that you have acted in this desirable way in the past. It may have been in situations that you have previously overlooked or dismissed as unimportant, but it still counts. You have behaved as if you already had the belief in yourself. Armed with this knowledge, you're well on the way to establishing the new positive belief.

4. *Act the part.* Commit to behaving in future as if you already have the belief. This may sound like play-acting and, in truth, that's what it is. But if, to use the present example, you consistently act the part of somebody who believes that they can handle whatever life may throw at them, then in time the act becomes reality. You're no longer just behaving as if you have the belief – you actually have it.

5. *Use positive affirmations.* Reinforce the belief with simple strong statements repeated regularly to yourself. Just as negative self-talk has played a major part in reinforcing limiting beliefs, so positive statements can significantly boost those new enabling beliefs you wish to advance. Don't just use affirmations when you are under pressure, give yourself the benefit of them at other times too. Speak them out loud if you are able to without risk of being locked up. Start and finish the day with these statements of faith in yourself – 'I can cope with whatever the day throws at me. I'm calm, patient, competent.'

6. *Record your progress.* Keeping a diary is an excellent way to assist your progress towards new self-belief. It

can provide hard evidence of all the positive steps you have taken – steps that might otherwise be overlooked. And it offers another vehicle for giving yourself the benefit of strong affirming statements. You may find that such statements when written are more powerful than when repeated to yourself.

achieve your goals

Goals can be a double-edged sword as far as self-esteem is concerned. On the one hand they are an important element in building your self-esteem – deciding what you want from your life and setting yourself on the path to achieving it. They are an essential part of that sense of control of your fortunes that is so important to feeling at ease with yourself. Without goals you are adrift in the ocean, at the mercy of every wind and current.

But, quite clearly, it is not enough just to set yourself goals; you also have to achieve them. Goals not met are a potent source of damage to your self-esteem, giving rise to anxiety, frustration and self-recrimination. And there are various reasons why we might fail to achieve our goals – absence of realism, lack of attention to the means of achievement, loss of momentum along the way. In this chapter we will look at how to gain the pluses while avoiding the minuses.

exercise

Let's start by getting some raw material you can work on. Jot down half a dozen things that you want to do with your life, but for one reason or another you have not yet been able to achieve. Don't worry too much at this stage about how well-expressed they are or whether they represent the most important of your life objectives. I would like to spend the rest of this section looking at how you might refine them and carry them forward.

For the purposes of illustration let me introduce you to a fictitious individual we'll call Mike. His initial list of goals is as follows:

- to renovate an old house in France and go there to live;
- to become more comfortable in situations where I have to talk to people;
- to run a marathon;
- to get a promotion in my job;
- to be less of a perfectionist;
- to learn to relax.

These items are clearly different in character, ranging from one-off activity to a complete change of lifestyle. But without additional work, all will remain in the realm of daydreams. So, how should Mike set about turning them into tools that are up to the job of getting him from where he is now to where he wants to be?

There are five requirements he needs to bear in mind: *clarity*, *realism*, *economy*, *activity* and *means*. Writers and trainers love mnemonics for this type of thing and I'm no exception. So the mnemonic on this occasion is CREAM.

essential elements
clarity

If a goal is going to be of value, it needs to be clear. It should answer the following questions:

■ What exactly am I aiming to achieve?
■ By when am I hoping to achieve it?
■ How will I know if I have got there?

Several of Mike's goals are currently too vague to be useful. Take number one as an example; what does he mean by *go and live there*? Is he thinking of it as a retirement aim or is he hoping to earn his living in France? The answer could make a great difference to the timescale and the complexity of the project. And if he is thinking about the second option, how does that fit with his aim of getting a promotion in his current job? What about the second item on the list? What does he want to do that he feels he can't do now? Is it about making small talk at parties, giving a formal presentation, or handling difficult situations such as making complaints or disciplining a member of staff? Without greater clarity he will lack the focus to attack his perceived weaknesses and to gain the satisfaction that comes from achieving his goals. You don't have to go overboard trying to achieve total precision, but do make sure that goals are specific enough that you are able to identify the activities necessary to bring about their achievement, and that they have a clear end point and associated deadline.

realism

Setting goals that are too demanding and are consequently not met, may lead to you damaging rather than enhancing your self-esteem. On the other hand, there is nothing to be gained by defining targets that can be achieved without any effort. Deep down you won't be fooled by the illusion of progress. The trick has to be about immediate goals that are just out of your reach. It's a matter of having to stretch to achieve them but not to saddle yourself with aspirations that will be impossible to meet. Does that mean then that if you want to preserve your self-esteem you can't have a grand objective – an aspiration that is well beyond your current abilities? No it doesn't, provided you break down your main objective into sub-goals and work towards your grand vision in manageable stages.

Take Mike's fourth goal as an example. He wants to run a marathon, but to date he has never run further than a mile. His goal of running 26 miles is way beyond his current capabilities, but he can get there if he builds up to it in graded stages, taking his mileage from one to two, to four, to six and so on. All the time his main objective is there in front of him, but he is working towards it in realistic steps and gaining the sense of progress and achievement with each advance. Getting from where he is now to where he wants to be is a hell of a leap, but each of the staged increases in his mileage is eminently achievable. Of course, I've chosen an easy example. What I have described is a pretty standard way of building physical fitness and endurance. But my argument is that you can use a similar approach whatever the challenge – realistic steps towards a finally achievable goal.

economy

Don't set yourself too many goals within a given time period. You won't be able to give them all the necessary attention, and the effect could be the same as setting over-ambitious goals. If Mike tries to embark on all six of his goals simultaneously he may risk the lot.

activity

Express your goals in positive and active terms. Try to frame them as things you will do rather than things that will happen to you. So, rather than Mike resolving to be promoted in the next 12 months, it might be better for him to frame his goal along the lines of: 'to demonstrate that I have the skills to work at a higher level'. The things he will do to meet this revised objective are no different, but at least its achievement is within his control. Whether or not he is promoted could be dependent on a whole range of factors: somebody else leaving; a restructuring plan that might open up or close down opportunities; an interviewer's preference for another candidate. Mike cannot control any of these, so if he leaves his goal as initially expressed he risks pinning achievement, and with that some of his self-belief, on the actions of others. Stick as far as possible with the things that are in your hands.

means

The most important thing to bear in mind when you are setting goals is the means by which you are going to achieve them – your action plan for getting there. This is likely to involve the identification of sub-goals. It may mean learning new skills or strengthening certain attributes and personal qualities such as patience; determination; flexibility; objectivity.

Let's consider some of the means that Mike might identify in relation to his goal of living in France. He decides that before he can make any concrete moves he will need to:

▓ discuss the aim with his partner, to ensure they share the same level of commitment to the project;
▓ research ways in which they could make an income while living in France;
▓ improve language skills;
▓ acquire some of the DIY skills he will need;
▓ work out how they will deal with a big shift in status and income.

Each of these will raise further questions. For example, what are the DIY skills he will require? What differences are there in French building techniques that might require skills not normally taught in this country? How will he acquire these?

Answering the questions will lead to the formation of an action plan for each of the elements of his overall goal. No rocket science here, just a methodical approach and the knowledge that each step is essential to the achievement of the main goal.

strengthening personal qualities

The prospect of changing long-standing traits may appear difficult, but it is quite possible provided you set about it in the right way. Let's assume you have decided that one of the qualities you need to work upon is determination. A general resolution to be more determined is too nebulous to have a great chance of success. So narrow it down. Identify a limited number of instances in which your resolve is most likely to flag – situations involving conflict, for example. Now make a decision that for the next week you will show more determination in such situations. Reward yourself for successfully achieving that limited change of behaviour and extend the period for a month. Once more, reward yourself for sticking to it. Then look for other situations in which increased determination is desirable and work on them in the same way, using your success so far to motivate yourself and reinforce belief in your ability to make the change. Taking the behaviour change in graded steps like this gives you something to get your teeth into and makes it achievable.

overcoming obstacles

As you move towards achievement of your goals you will in all probability have to deal with obstacles in your way. They may come from other individuals and take the form of bullying, criticism or interference. Alternatively, they may be features of your lifestyle or work situation – for instance overload, stress or disorganisation. You cannot predict with certainty every hindrance you may face, but it is useful at goal-setting stage to be aware of the obvious ones, so that you can be ready with strategies to overcome them.

to share or not to share?

Some writers and coaches will insist that you should share your goals with a supportive friend or even make a public commitment to them, while others maintain that personal goals are best kept confidential. There are pluses and minuses to both approaches. Once you have made a public commitment you are under greater pressure to deliver. This may mean that you're more likely to succeed, but it may carry the disadvantage of greater stress and rigidity. Having declared your intentions, it is more difficult to make amendments to the goal in the light of changing circumstances. It can become a matter of do it or be seen to fail. Sharing goals also provides you with the possibility of support when the going gets tough, although this too can be a double-edged sword. Well-meaning friends may lack the commitment that you feel towards the objective and with the best of motives can talk you out of it. When Mike talks to colleagues about his marathon ambitions and the difficulty he is having with his training, he gets comments like, 'Are you sure you're up to it?' and 'You're not getting any younger.' 'There was a man your age who dropped dead in the London Marathon last year.' And in addition to our well-meaning friends there are the people who just don't want us to succeed – those who are jealous or who aim to bolster their own low self-esteem by seeking out failure in others.

At the end of the day it boils down to your own personality and the nature of the goals you have chosen. Keeping them private gives them a special quality and possibly makes for a greater sense of achievement when you are successful. Sharing them opens up the possibility of drawing on additional resources, but may subject you to external discouragement.

exercise

Having looked at some of the things that need to be borne in mind when setting goals, go back to the rough list you jotted down earlier. Ask yourself:

- Is it clear what I want to achieve and by when?
- Have I framed my goals in such a way that I will know when I have got there?
- Are my goals adequately stretching but not unrealistic?
- Am I able to break down each goal into those sub-tasks that will need to be completed to ensure its achievement?
- Can I identify the skills and qualities I will need to work upon and the obstacles I may have to overcome?
- Have I paid sufficient attention to timescale and the conflicting demands of my various goals?

Work up action plans for your goals in the light of these questions.

getting there

OK, you have worked out what you will need to do, but that's not enough to get you there without some attention to the journey. We can liken the process of moving towards your goals to that of climbing a mountain. When you set out, you can see your objective, the summit, clearly in front of you. It appears almost within touching distance. You flog away for a long time but it never seems to get any closer. And there are valleys and gullies that weren't visible to you at the start. It's easy to become discouraged. Here are five points that will help ensure you are able to keep going:

1. *Deal with the challenge in bite-sized chunks.* We have already talked about breaking your main goals down into the constituent tasks needed to complete them, but you may need to reduce them to much smaller levels of achievement. For example, one of the sub-goals for Mike's plan to live in France is to improve his ability to speak French, and that in itself is a considerable task. He needs a sense of momentum to keep him going and so it's important to find measurable chunks of progress that are meaningful and to aim for these while not neglecting the more distant objective. Mastering the vocabulary and grammar to deal with just one new situation might be seen as a small but significant step towards the goal of living and working in France. There is a corny but accurate jingle that goes: Life by the yard is apt to be hard. Life by the inch is a bit of a cinch.

2. *Review progress regularly.* Checking to see how you are doing against the grand scheme of things is the next part of the strategy. Keep yourself on track by earmarking a regular time – weekly or monthly – when you will review how you are doing and look ahead to the next steps. The use of simple 'to do' lists can help you in setting your weekly or monthly agenda and there is great satisfaction to be gained when you are able to cross items off the list.

3. *Reward yourself along the way.* The distant reward to be gained from achievement of the final objective may not be enough to keep you going when things get tough. Recognise and reward smaller elements of progress. It may be that you give yourself a treat for reaching significant milestones, or simply that you pat yourself on the back, perhaps by way of an entry in your diary when you take smaller steps forward.

4. *Be prepared to explore alternative routes.* Returning once more to my mountain-climbing analogy, the

route to the summit will not always be the one you foresaw when you started out. Ploughing on regardless of the developing situation can lead to disappointment and failure. So remain flexible. It may be necessary for you to modify your approach, even to aim for a different summit. And be prepared to move sideways or even downwards from time to time in order get around obstacles.

5. *Enjoy the journey.* Driving yourself along with your sights set too rigidly on the final outcome is not the way to feel good about yourself. The inevitable setbacks will bring frustration and the destination when it is reached is likely to feel like an anticlimax. Your self-esteem is more likely to benefit if you loosen up a bit, take things as they come and even enjoy finding solutions to the difficulties. Remaining steady in the face of increasing challenge is the same as moving forward, and deciding to change your direction does not mean that you have failed.

change your perspective

We have already looked at a number of techniques for shifting our negative attitudes and distorted thinking: affirmations, questioning, acknowledging achievements, recasting beliefs. In this chapter we will look at several more ways of introducing positive thinking that can have a very significant effect on performance and the way you view yourself.

visualisation

Visualisation is best known in the sports arena. All top athletes and sportspeople use a tactic of mental rehearsal in which they visualise themselves achieving the standards they are training for – running that bit faster, moving smoothly and effortlessly, playing the perfect game. There is no doubt that it works, and can apply equally to other forms of human endeavour. Routinely picturing yourself succeeding at whatever you set out to do serves to remove psychological limitations you have placed on yourself through previous perceptions of failure and negative self-talk. It has been shown that during the mental rehearsal of visualisation, two-thirds of the brain activity is the same as when the activity is carried out for real. Through it a positive mental image is created, which counteracts the negative messages we have been inclined to feed ourselves and reduces the anxiety we might otherwise feel. We are enabled to approach the activity with an attitude closely resembling that arising from successful previous experience. Needless to say, this can have a potent effect on our performance and the way we feel about ourselves when faced with challenging situations.

The everyday life activities that particularly lend themselves to being improved by visualisation are those that involve an element of performance or difficult interaction. These are often among the situations most feared by people whose self-esteem has not been high. They include such things as: the requirement to give a presentation or a speech; attendance at an interview; challenging interpersonal situations such as a difficult meeting with one's boss or confronting a problem with a work colleague; making a complaint or a request in a hostile environment.

how to visualise

Visualisation is most effective if you are relaxed when you do it, so you might want to go through a conscious relaxation routine before you start. Some people claim that it works best if practised just prior to a night's sleep, although if you normally experience difficulty shutting off your thoughts and quickly falling asleep, it is best to avoid such timing. Once you are relaxed, you can put your imagination to work, not only on the images of the event you seek to visualise, but on the associated words and feelings too.

Let's use as an example a tricky meeting at which you have to discipline a difficult member of your team. Mentally rehearse all aspects of the interview you will have with them. Visualise the way you will talk to them, the words you will use, even your confident body language. Picture yourself handling the situation successfully and assertively. Visualise the event not just as a sort of slide show, but as a dynamic enactment with you as the central participant. Don't ignore the anxiety that would be a normal accompaniment to such a meeting. Sense it, but visualise yourself overcoming it. You remain relaxed and in control, breathing calm and regular, no hint of becoming angry or flustered. You are using the right words in the way that you would like to. Your body language demonstrates confidence and assurance. And perhaps most important of all, be conscious of the feelings you have about yourself. Recognise and appreciate the strong sense of self-worth that comes with your assured performance.

Remember that visualisation is a supplement to, not a replacement for, other preparation. You still need to do the normal work in preparation for whatever the challenge might be. If possible, run a visualisation several times to make a real difference. Don't let any negative elements come into the picture – if they do, gently move them away. Don't dwell on them or seek to force them out, allowing anger and frustration to develop.

Visualisation is not only useful in facing up to challenging and feared activities. You can use it to lift your performance in all manner of individual events and regular occurrences or as a way of maintaining motivation and reinforcing belief in your ability to reach longer-term goals.

anchoring

Anchoring is a technique that makes use of associations in order to help us cope with situations that might otherwise have the potential to make us anxious, fearful, lacking in self-belief. It has some similarities to visualisation, but instead of rehearsing a future event, it draws on the resources of positive past experiences and uses anchors – conscious associations that serve to call forth those resources when needed.

We make unconscious associations all the time. Some of them can be very powerful at recapturing past experiences and the thoughts and feelings linked to them. A snatch of music, a particular image or a long-forgotten smell may not only bring back memories of an event in your life, but more particularly cause you to experience once more the strong emotions associated with it. Such triggers can call up positive or negative feelings. I'm sure you will have met people who proclaim a negative response to what they describe as a 'hospital smell'. They associate certain antiseptic smells with feelings of apprehension or perhaps distress that they were experiencing when they encountered them on a previous occasion. Similarly, anything that sounds like a dentist's drill will have many of us stuffing our fingers in our ears in horror.

Anchoring is about generating conscious links that conjure up positive rather than negative feelings, allowing us to revisit experiences associated with high self-esteem, and to utilise those feelings in current situations. The way to set about creating these links is as follows:

1. Find an event in your memory when you felt good about yourself – calm, confident and in control. It doesn't matter too much what the situation was, but it should be one that was unequivocally positive – no conflicting messages.

2. Select a word or short phrase that you will use as a link to the positive feelings characterised by this situation. The phrase will be one that you repeat internally to yourself when you wish to call up the positive response. It should therefore be simple and memorable. You might, for example, choose the phrase 'calm and confident'.

3. Choose a physical gesture that you will use as a conscious link in conjunction with the word or phrase.

It should be a distinctive gesture – not one that you use as you go about your normal daily life, but it shouldn't be anything outlandish. You need to be able to use it without attracting attention to yourself when you're in need of a boost in self-belief. So, patting yourself on the top of the head is probably not the best idea. Try something like pressing your thumb against your little finger or making a fist with your thumb tucked inside.

4. If possible, select an image that you can associate with the positive experience you are going to link up to. For example, if the event was a sporting achievement, your image might be a trophy or a medal, if it was a celebration of some other form you might pick a champagne glass.

5. Having selected your anchors it is now time to revisit the positive experience and establish the links. Make yourself comfortable in a pleasant and quiet place where you are not likely to be interrupted. Ensure that you are suitably relaxed and are not preoccupied by extraneous thoughts or concerns. If you have a regular relaxation routine you might like to go through it first. Now start to revisit the positive experience, recapturing everything you can about it – the words used, the sounds, smells, sensations and, particularly, the way you felt. Really enjoy the experience once again. As you do so – at the point that you are feeling really good – introduce your anchors. Say your chosen word or phrase silently to yourself, make the gesture, picture the image. And repeat them several times if possible, in the same order, while you continue to relive and enjoy the past positive experience.

6. Having established the links, test them out by saying the word internally, making the gesture and calling up the image. Does this routine recapture for you the sense of well-being you experienced in the original situation? If not, go through step five again – perhaps

repeating it two or three more times – to ensure a really strong association. Be sure to relax beforehand and get yourself completely into the situation before you introduce the anchors.

7. The final step is to use the trigger devices to call up the sense of well-being when you need it. You might like to think in advance of common situations you face when such a resource could be handy, so that you are prepared to use it when the need arises. However, don't hold the technique in reserve for too long. The sooner you start to use it in real-life situations the better. Go through the trigger devices as you did when you established and tested them – say the word internally, make the gesture and call up the image. You may find that just one of them is enough for you to get the boost that makes all the difference to your ability to cope with what otherwise would be a difficult situation for you.

If you don't achieve success at the first go, keep trying and repeat the routine of establishing the links. Once you have successfully used the technique, you might like to introduce new routines. You could, for example, use it for situations when you want to show more determination. The procedure is the same. Choose the past situation when you experienced the feelings you wish to replicate, choose the triggers, establish the links, test them, use them.

reframing

There is always more than one way of looking at a situation, and reframing is about seeking out the positives rather than emphasising the negatives. By altering the frame that you put upon an event you can change your responses to it. To use the old cliché, it's a case of seeing the glass as half full rather than half empty. I am not suggesting that it is always simple – in some situations you will have to work hard to tease out a more positive construction, but you can do it, and it can make a great difference to your attitude and performance.

Reframing doesn't make problems disappear, but it can turn them into challenges. Neither is it a matter of pretending to yourself. It is a rare event from which absolutely nothing positive can be drawn. There are countless examples of individuals who have suffered the most extreme of personal disasters – serious illness, disablement, wrongful imprisonment – yet have still been able to use the experience to learn about themselves and to gain new directions in life. If seeking out the positives from the most negative of experiences is possible, then how much easier to use conscious reframing to deal with those day-to-day occasions when we are inclined to punish and belittle ourselves. Here are some examples of how a more positive construction can be put on a negative thought or statement:

'Why can I never manage to get it right first time?'
'My ability to return to a task and make improvements is a strength.'

'I really struggled with that assignment.'
'That assignment taught me some new lessons and I'll be more effective in future as a result.'

'All the senior managers are attending my presentation. I'm petrified I'll make a fool of myself.'
'This presentation will give me the chance to demonstrate my capabilities to the people who matter.'

Reframing will take a bit of practice, so be prepared to stick with it, and remain on the lookout for any occasion when you can use the techniques to cancel out negative thoughts. One word of warning, however. Take care not to use reframing as a means of inventing excuses for procrastination or avoidance.

acceptance

All the strategies we have looked at aim to attack the negative thoughts you have generated about yourself, but there are occasions when you can usefully adopt an approach that seems to run counter to everything I have said so far. Rather than challenging some weaknesses, it may pay simply to accept them. It's a case of changing what you can and accepting what you can't. Used at the right time, a strategy of simply accepting weaknesses, recognising that you are an imperfect human being like everyone else on the planet, is rather like a judo move. It throws your strategies of defence and concealment off balance and, rather than weakening you further, allows you to emerge feeling stronger. No longer do you have to battle away trying to deny perceived shortcomings or to hide them from yourself and others. When you accept them, they no longer weigh you down.

Acceptance is a strategy that fits with that general sense of unconditional self-esteem that I referred to in Chapter 1 – liking and respecting yourself simply for being you, with all your weaknesses and idiosyncrasies. I must stress that you should not use this approach to accept or acknowledge any feelings of general uselessness. It should only be about accepting specific failings that may not be amenable to some of the other techniques we have explored. And it should most certainly not be an occasion for self-deprecation or any other form of punishment. Accepting specific weaknesses with dignity and self-respect can free up resources to root out other manifestations of negativity, and your self-esteem is not weakened but strengthened.

detachment

In this section I will be referring to techniques such as meditation. They differ from the strategies above in that rather than seeking to address your distorted thinking or the influences upon you, they take you into territory where self-esteem is unimportant because the self is unimportant. The sense of peace, harmony and heightened awareness that one can achieve by stepping outside the petty concerns of normal life has a salutary effect long after the meditation is finished. I have not the space here to enter upon a detailed examination of meditation techniques and in any event I would not wish to present myself as an expert. Here, however, is a simple mind-calming routine for those readers who have not previously tried these techniques and would like a taster. There are numerous books and tapes available should you wish to go further, or you might like to join a class.

mind-calming routine

Ideally, find a pleasant location where you can be quiet and are unlikely to be interrupted. Complete privacy does not have to be guaranteed, however. You aren't going to be doing anything that invites ridicule if you are interrupted. Adopt a comfortable but balanced posture. If you are seated in a chair, make sure it is an upright one (not an easy chair or sofa). Your back should be straight with a slight inward curve in the lower back, feet flat on the floor and hands resting gently in your lap. Don't sit rigidly to attention, but be sure not to slump either. Let your back lengthen and widen, and your neck be free. Alternatively, you might wish to sit cross-legged or kneel on the floor with your bottom resting on your upturned feet. You can place a cushion under your buttocks to take the weight off your ankles if you wish. Again your back should be straight but not rigid. To help achieve a balanced posture imagine a plumb line alongside your body. It should pass through the lobe of your ear, the point of your shoulder and the top of your hip bone.

Close or half-close your eyes, letting the lids droop and relaxing your gaze. Breathe slowly through the nose and place the tongue gently against the palate so that your breath is slightly audible to you.

Now focus your attention on your feet. Take a long, slow, deep breath and, as you do so, visualise that the air you are breathing is being drawn in through the soles of your feet and is travelling all the way up your legs and lower body until it reaches your lungs. Picture this air as a fresh, cleansing, relaxing force as it passes through your body. And as it travels, it collects up all the stress and tension that it meets. Hold the breath with all the tensions it has gathered up for a mental count of four, then let it go in a long, low, deep sigh, and release with it all those pent up anxieties, stresses and tensions.

Continue to visualise your breath coming up from your feet in this way for several more inhalations and experience the muscular relaxation and sense of well-being in the areas you have imagined it passing through. Give particular attention to the stomach region, letting the breath soothe away any knots, anxieties or emotional tension.

When you feel you have attained a state of peace and relaxation in the lower part of your body, switch your attention to your hands. This time imagine the breath coming in through the tips of your fingers and travelling all the way up your arms and through your shoulders and the lower part of your neck before reaching the lungs. Picture it like the crystal clear waters of a mountain spring, and once again visualise it picking up any stresses and tensions it finds along the way. Pay particular attention to your shoulders and neck, which are especially susceptible to muscular tension. Hold the breath for a mental count of four and then release it with all its cargo of stress and unease. Repeat this part of the routine several times and experience the sense of wonderful relaxation in the upper part of your body.

Finally, turn your attention to the top of your head and imagine each inhalation coming in through your scalp. The soothing breath passes down through your brain, face, jaw and neck, collecting not only the muscular tension, but also all the anger, anxiety, niggling thoughts and empty mental chatter that is cluttering up your brain. And again you hold them all for a mental count of four before releasing them in a long, slow, deep sigh. With each breath you take, experience yourself letting go of all those negative thoughts and feelings that you have allowed to inhabit your body. You put them there, and you can let them go. Be aware of your mind gently emptying and moving into harmony with the rest of your body, peaceful and relaxed.

Now let your breathing fall into a slow, gentle rhythm, no longer holding your breath at any point nor directing your attention to particular parts of your body. Just slow, gentle breaths. Remain conscious of the gentle ebb and flow of your breathing and the peaceful emptiness of mind and body. You may find it helpful to use a mantra – just two or three words inwardly repeated over and over will do. Try *peace, harmony, balance*. Many people benefit from having a simple object on which they can focus their attention. It might be something like a candle, a flower, a smooth pebble. If you should find your attention wandering and thoughts coming into your mind, don't try to force them out, just gently let them go.

The next stage is one that might take a different form depending on your religious beliefs or deeply held convictions. Be prepared to adapt what I describe to fit your personal philosophy on life. *Just experience being*. Those gentle breaths of which you are still aware are the very essence of life, and you are completely at one with life, in harmony with the entire universe in whatever way you may choose to view it. You are part of something balanced, ordered and complete, as much a part of the universe as every other element that comprises it. As you experience just being – time, location and awareness of self become unimportant. You have stepped away from those petty concerns that preoccupy you in your daily life. You have discarded the anxieties and tensions that your brain has concocted. They are of no consequence. In their place you have a oneness with universal peace and harmony. You have left self behind.

Hold on to that wonderful sense of tranquillity for as long as you wish or are able to do so. Don't think, just experience. You may find yourself dispassionately observing yourself, as if from outside your body. When you are ready, let yourself return to the here and now, and feel the huge sense of well-being and capability that stays with you.

You won't always be able to achieve the same level of peace and detachment. If you are particularly anxious at the outset, you may find it difficult to dispel your chattering thoughts. But persist with your efforts; the pay-off is more than worth it. And don't stick with the simple routine I have described here. Adapt it to your own preferences, and read some of the widely available material on meditation, or try one of the many tapes. Join a yoga or meditation class to take further the benefits of physical and mental harmony.

assert yourself

assertiveness, aggression and passivity

Of all the reasons behind self-criticism and feelings of worthlessness, some of the most common are to do with the belief that we have failed to stand up for ourselves when the occasion demanded; that rather than controlling a situation, we have allowed the situation to control us; that we have been bullied or manipulated by others. The ability to assert ourselves is then an important element in feeling good about ourselves.

There is a common tendency to view assertiveness as no more than the ability to stand up for oneself. This limited interpretation risks confusing assertiveness with aggression, and it is important to dispel the confusion at the outset. Aggressive behaviour can also be portrayed as standing up for oneself, but it does so at the expense of others. It is a matter of getting one's own way regardless. Assertiveness, on the other hand, proceeds from a strong awareness of one's own needs and entitlements but does not neglect those of other people. And there is so much more to assertiveness. It implies honesty, tact, flexibility, effective communication, the ability to listen. In short, assertiveness is about all-round proactive interpersonal behaviour.

Acting assertively means:

- ▓ being open and honest with yourself and others;
- ▓ standing up for your own rights but respecting the rights of others;
- ▓ saying what you mean;
- ▓ sticking to the point and refusing to be sidetracked;
- ▓ dealing appropriately with conflict situations;
- ▓ being prepared to say no;
- ▓ making clear what you want, but not riding roughshod over others.

Aggressive behaviour means:

- ▓ refusing to consider the point of view of others;
- ▓ having your own way regardless of others' needs;
- ▓ abusing and intimidating others;
- ▓ making other people feel small;
- ▓ bullying or manipulating others into doing things they don't want to do.

Aggression may get you your own way, but it doesn't provide you with a means of working positively with others or finding solutions to difficult interpersonal problems. It won't help you deal with justified criticism or recognise the occasions when you are more likely to achieve a positive outcome through tact and flexibility.

We commonly think of an aggressive person as the classic loud, insensitive bully. But this is not the only form of aggression. It can also come in a quieter, more insidious form. Indirect aggression uses such tactics as ignoring or ostracising people, ridiculing them or making jokes at their expense. The indirect aggressor may behave in a two-faced fashion – pleasant to your face, vicious behind your back.

Assertiveness is often portrayed as a middle way between passive and aggressive behaviour, but this is not entirely accurate. Aggression and passivity are both essentially low self-esteem behaviours – limited belief in self and either excessive respect or absence of respect for others. People who resort to aggression are possibly attempting to bolster themselves at the expense of others, while those who display passive behaviour may be taking the line that only by suppressing their own needs can they gain acceptance.

Passive behaviour is about:

▓ avoiding conflict at all costs;
▓ bottling up your feelings and preferences;
▓ agreeing with others for fear of upsetting them;
▓ not saying what you want;
▓ apologising unnecessarily;
▓ saying yes when you would rather say no, and then complaining to others about being put upon.

For passive don't read easy-going. Passivity tends to be accompanied by a lot of anger. You feel you should speak up about the bullying behaviour of your boss, but you don't. You want to say no to an unreasonable request, but you don't. If you constantly bottle up your own views, you can get to the point where you scarcely know what they are any more. But you are still angry – with yourself and with the person you believe to be trampling on you. And this anger finds its way through to lowered general self-esteem.

There are, however, times when you may decide to let things pass, and do so without anger or self-deprecation. These may be occasions when you judge that challenging an issue is really not worth the hassle, or when you can take the heat out of a difficult situation by refusing to rise to the bait. There might even be instances where you are moved for tactical reasons to drop in an apology for something that was not your fault. Provided that your motivation arises from a judgement that such actions will lead to the sort of solution you require, rather than from an inability to assert yourself, and provided also that you are able to engage in them without damage to your self-belief, then I would argue that your behaviour has all the hall-marks of assertiveness.

While we may have a tendency towards a certain type of behaviour – passive, aggressive, assertive – it won't necessarily be exclusive. We all have a variety of life roles in which we play quite different parts. You may find that there are some aspects of your life in which you are much more assertive than others. There may be particular people who seem to bring out the aggressive streak in you, or situations in which you are routinely passive. Observe too, how some people swing wildly between extremes – excessively subservient towards those in authority, bullying or manipulative towards those they perceive as weaker.

So, there is nothing fixed about these different ways of dealing with others. The most important point to appreciate is that aggression, passivity and assertiveness are all learned behaviours and as such are open to change. It is entirely achiev-able for you to behave in a more assertive way, and in so doing to boost and protect your self-esteem. In the remainder of this chapter we will look at ways of doing so. We will examine tech-niques for assertive interactions, then look at handling criti-cism, and finally consider ways of dealing with bullies.

But first, just spend a few minutes reflecting on your own patterns of assertiveness, or lack of it. Who and where are the problem people and what are the problem situations? You will find this exercise more useful if you jot down your responses rather than just thinking about them.

exercise

1. Who are the people or types of people with whom you have difficulty being assertive? List those who come to mind and ask yourself what it is about them that makes for the diffi-

culty. There are likely to be the obvious things like power, authority, physical presence; but there may be other things that are not so readily evident. Why is it difficult to be assertive with builders? What is it about that woman in the Accounts Office that has me cringing and putting up with abuse?

2. What are the situations in which you generally find it hard to be assertive? Again jot down those you can think of. Are the most difficult situations always associated with the most difficult people? Are there possibly associations with previous occasions when you feel you performed poorly? Do problems tend to arise in circumstances that are unfamiliar or where you are unsure about what is expected of you?

3. Now think of occasions when you have been able to be assertive. Are there any things you especially notice about these? What were the things that helped you to be assertive? Did you prepare yourself for the encounter in any particular way? How did you feel when you were able to be assertive?

assertiveness techniques

If you genuinely feel good about yourself, you are more able to be open and honest with others, to respect differing opinions without feeling threatened by them, and to stand your ground when the occasion demands. In that respect, then, most of the ground we have covered in the book so far will be of value. And some of the techniques we have examined are especially useful in helping you deal with those occasions when your assertiveness skills are really put to the test:

▓ Visualisation allows you to prepare yourself mentally for a difficult encounter.

▓ Anchoring enables you to call up resources when you need them.

■ Affirmations and reframing help you to counteract the negative self-talk that can steer you into passive or aggressive behaviour.

Here are some more strategies to ensure that you can handle difficult situations calmly and directly, getting your point across and refusing to be browbeaten, but without descending into aggression.

learn your lines

In tricky situations we may know full well what it is we want to say, but somehow it doesn't come out as we had intended. The difficult request fizzles out in the face of a hostile reception, the complaint turns into an apology. The first rule for ensuring that this doesn't happen is to prepare in advance what you want to say – with the emphasis on simplicity, clarity and directness – and then to rehearse it thoroughly, to the point that you are able to deliver your message confidently and control any feelings of nervousness or anger. Prepare what you want to say in four parts:

1. *An explanation of the situation.* Keep this short and to the point – if possible no more than a couple of sentences. If you're dealing with a complex matter, try to pull out just the essential information. The more detail you present, the easier it is to be sidetracked. Don't go in for elaborate introductions or justification of your position.

2. *Your feelings about the situation.* Letting the other person know how you feel allows you to present yourself as open and yet in control. You can say for example that you feel very angry, rather than demonstrating your anger with all the consequent loss of control and potential for retaliation. Confine your

description to what you feel and don't introduce an accusatory element. So it's a matter of, 'I feel really upset about this,' not, 'You've really upset me.' However, it may be appropriate at this stage to acknowledge the other person's feelings with remarks such as, 'I realise this is difficult for you too.'

3. *What you wish to happen.* This should be clear and direct but not unreasonable. Depending on the circumstances, it might be appropriate to indicate some flexibility in your requirements, but again be sure not to dilute your message with apologies or justifications.

4. *The benefits.* The final element is to point out the benefits to the other person of following your request. They should be presented as positives that arise from complying rather than negatives resulting from non-compliance. An example might be, 'This will make me feel more confident about doing business with your company in future,' rather than, 'If you don't agree, I'll take my business elsewhere.'

Following this structure will allow you to present yourself clearly and assertively. But before you move on to rehearsing your piece, consider two more things. Do you need a fall-back position in the event that you don't get exactly what you want from the encounter? And is there value in having some negative consequences held in reserve that you can use as threats if your attempt to sell the positive benefits doesn't work?

the scratched record

This is a technique with which you may not at first be entirely comfortable. But it does work, and can be extremely effective when dealing with pushy or unreasonable individuals who are attempting to browbeat you. The term comes from a distinctly old technology of yesteryear when a scratch on a vinyl LP would cause the same snatch of music to be endlessly repeated. And that is exactly what you do. You select a succinct statement that clearly summarises your position and use it repeatedly with the minimum of elaboration until you get your message across. We're into the territory of political interviews here, and that's the reason you might not be comfortable. But remember, this isn't a technique for winning popularity competitions. It's for keeping you on track when you're in danger of being bullied or manipulated into agreeing to something that is against your interests. Here is the way the exchange might go:

Boss: 'I've got to ask you to cancel your day off next week. I've had a call from the regional manager. He's coming in that day and I need you around in case there are any difficult queries.'
You: 'I'm sorry, I have an important commitment that I can't alter. I need to take the day off.'
Boss: 'But you must realise how difficult it's going to be. You'll have to make some other arrangements.'
You: 'I understand that it will be difficult, but I have an important commitment that I can't alter. I need to take the day off.'
Boss: 'Look! You're a vital part of the team, we all need to be prepared for this visit.'
You: 'I'm happy to do everything possible to prepare for it, but I have a commitment I can't alter. I need to take the day off.'

And so on... Notice how the respondent doesn't simply trot out the statement ungarnished, but throws in additional remarks to indicate that they understand the other's point of view. It may help to have a fall-back position – a possible solution you can throw into the pot if the situation degenerates into complete deadlock – but don't let yourself be manoeuvred into using it too early.

remember your body language

Body language communicates more powerfully than the words we use. If what you are saying is contradicted by your eyes, hands and posture, then no matter how well you have chosen your words, they will be overlooked. So, if you are going to present yourself in an assertive manner, it is vital that you give these things some attention.

eyes

The importance of good eye contact cannot be overestimated. We look to the eyes to confirm whether what is being said can be relied upon as accurate. Are they telling the truth, exaggerating, afraid, sincere, angry, genuinely sorry, truly enthusiastic, ashamed? Absence of eye contact is associated with having something to hide. People who fail to meet our eyes sufficiently may be regarded as shifty or untrustworthy. In fact, low levels of eye contact may result from nothing more than shyness. If you are affected, then you will need to work on making more frequent eye contact a normal feature of conversation. Some people find that it helps to practise speaking in front of a mirror. But don't go overboard on eye contact – too much is as discomforting as too little. Intense eyeballing may be associated with aggression.

In a one-to-one conversation aim at maintaining eye contact for between a half and two-thirds of the time. A useful little technique for achieving this is to shift your attention between three points on the other person's face. First focus on their right eye for three of four seconds, then move to their left eye for roughly the same period, and finally switch your attention to the point of their chin. Then it's back to the right eye, left eye and so on. It may feel rather artificial at first, but the other person won't notice anything unusual, and in quite a short time you should find that you are applying a three-point focus quite naturally and automatically.

When speaking to a number of people, take care that you are

not focusing on just one or two individuals. Try to sweep your audience with your gaze. If you are dealing with just a small number of people, try to make eye contact with all of them, not just those who may be smiling or signifying their approval in some way.

arms, legs and posture

How we move and hold our limbs has a considerable impact on the way we appear to others. Jerky movements, nervous mannerisms, fidgeting and fiddling with objects such as pens or fashion accessories are all signs of unease. Smoothness and fluidity of movement demonstrates assertiveness and control. Stressful situations bring out all our nervous mannerisms, but you can do something to ease the problem. When you use visualisation techniques to help prepare for a difficult situation, make sure that you incorporate movement into the scenario that you call up. Picture yourself moving in a smooth, calm and relaxed manner, your actions complementing your confident words.

If you're inclined to gesticulate or display nervous hand movements you may want to practise speaking while sitting on your hands. Should you be concerned that nervousness will cause your hands to shake, place them together, one gently cupped in the other, but don't clasp them too tightly or wring them. And try to keep your hands away from your face. It generally signals anxiety.

A compact posture – arms tucked in, feet and knees together shows submissiveness. Adopt a more open and expansive posture to radiate confidence and assertiveness. Not only will it send signals to others, it will make you feel better too. Folded arms are another closed posture – a classic sign of protectiveness – indicating a buttoned up desire to hold oneself in check or a wish to be somewhere else. Try to make sure also that your general posture is balanced and relaxed – neither hunched, slumped nor rigidly held to attention. The first two signal defeat, the third sends the same sort of signals as the folded arms. It is generally the case that a person who is standing can command greater authority than when they are sitting down, but this will not be the case if the standing posture is accompanied by signs of discomfort such as fidgeting or shifting from foot to foot. Better to sit or perch and feel relaxed than to stand and radiate tension.

act the part

This is a technique we have encountered earlier, but it bears repeating here. Many people who appear outwardly calm and confident in difficult and stressful situations will own up to a degree of pre-performance nervousness and apprehension. What they do is to act the part. And you can do that too. Even though you may have doubts about your capacity to be assertive, you can give yourself the edge by resolving that you will at least act the part. It's remarkable how, when you throw yourself into the role, pretence can rapidly give way to the real thing.

deal with criticism

Criticism can present one of the greatest challenges to our assertiveness and general self-esteem. I am sure you can recall occasions when a few words of censure have cut you to the quick, and have remained with you for a long time afterwards. So, what happens when somebody criticises you? Do you:

- ▧ counter-attack by raising their own shortcomings;
- ▧ make flippant remarks;
- ▧ feel like bursting into tears;
- ▧ go away and sulk?

These are just a few of many common reactions to an experience that nobody finds entirely comfortable. They are all defensive and low self-esteem responses. Everybody gets criticised at some time. It may arise from the most caring and constructive of motives – concern for our well-being, desire to help us change some perceived ineffective behaviour. Alternatively, it may be governed by vindictiveness and negativity – jealousy, anger, feelings of inferiority. Constructive criticism aims to change your behaviour. With destructive criticism the target is you.

Unfortunately, our initial response to both sorts is the same. We behave as if we are under attack – inappropriately, of course, because until we have listened to and analysed what is being said, we do not know whether what we are experiencing is an attack or a favour. There are four less than satisfactory ways of dealing with criticism. We can ignore it, throw it back, deflect it or be defeated by it.

ignoring it

At first glance, ignoring criticism might seem to be an assertive strategy and protective of self-esteem, but used as an habitual response it is a rigidly defensive stance that doesn't help us. An assertive person has the courage to face up to other people's perceptions of them and the ability to address issues raised. Those who make a practice of always ignoring criticism protect themselves at the cost of never learning from others or changing their behaviour. The ability to ignore criticism has its place. If you can identify and turn off the 'dripping taps' and those chronic critics who are just in the game of boosting their own self-image, then you can save yourself a lot of needless hassle. But don't seek to ignore as a sole strategy.

counter-attacking

The urge to counter-attack is most prevalent:

■ when we are aware that we have made a mistake and are already mentally chastising ourselves;

- ■ when we are feeling bruised;
- ■ when the criticism is accompanied by attack on character or an attempt to label us – 'you're lazy, thoughtless' etc.

Counter-attacking is seldom productive. Once again it's a response borne of weakness and feelings of vulnerability. While it might make you feel better briefly, the anger and emotion that goes into the response is likely to fuel longer-term resentment as well as escalating criticism into full-scale hostility and preventing you from hearing things that could be useful. Counter-attackers tend to make a habit of it regardless of the validity of the criticism or the scale of the problem.

deflection
Another defensive strategy. Instead of mounting a counter-attack, the deflector uses flippancy to dilute the impact of what is being said or seeks to attribute blame elsewhere.

defeat
This is the least assertive of all responses. People who are defeated by criticism take the view that others know best and that what is being said simply confirms their uselessness. They take all criticism as comment on their very existence and are unable to distinguish between the constructive and the malicious.

how to receive criticism

The first step in handling criticism in a confident and assertive manner is to remove the notion that it inevitably represents an attack on all that you stand for. While that assumption is in place you are likely to react inappropriately. Certainly, some criticism will be unjustified or vindictive, but you can only judge its validity by listening dispassionately and removing anger and emotion from your response. If you can do this, you will be in a better position to respond assertively to negative criticism and to draw the useful lessons from constructive criticism.

calm down

The sense of being under attack invokes what is often referred to as the 'fight or flight response'. This involuntary primitive reaction stems from a time when threats were inevitably of a physical nature and the options for us were either to turn and confront the aggressor or scamper to the nearest tree. The body prepares itself for action by releasing hormones and by an increase in heart rate and blood pressure, rapid, shallow breathing and increased perspiration. But in the modern world, the prospect of a physical response to a verbal attack is clearly inappropriate. Rather than a rapid physical response we need a calm rational one.

So when you feel yourself, literally, getting hot under the collar, what can you do to restore your cool? As I have said, the physical manifestations of 'fight or flight' are involuntary, but there is one that you can control fairly easily and use to bring yourself back to equilibrium. The element in question is breathing. Deliberately changing the pattern of rapid shallow breathing to one of measured deep breathing causes the other stress symptoms to subside and restores balance and calm to your body and mind. Take a long, slow, deep breath in, hold it to the mental count of four without straining, and release it in another long, slow breath. Pause for the mental count of four before taking the next inhalation. Continue with this regular deep breathing for as long as it takes for the symptoms to subside.

listen

The ability to listen is a skill we take for granted, but it's a talent that needs to be worked upon. We are inclined to regard it as a passive process, but it shouldn't be so. Being able to listen actively is a vital skill if you are to deal effectively with difficult interpersonal issues such as criticism. There are four basic rules for effective listening:

- Recognise that the other person has the right to a point of view. Their perception of the situation may be inaccurate, but then so might yours.
- Suspend judgement while they are talking – don't assume hostile motives. Once you signal your disagreement, you are liable to set off a defensive chain of response and counter-response leading to the loss of anything constructive.
- Reflect back what you believe the other person has said in order to confirm understanding. This is particularly necessary when receiving criticism as the anxiety that comes from feeling under attack can prevent you from accurately hearing what is being said.
- Seek clarification where necessary.

be objective

Try to step outside your feelings and view what is being said dispassionately. You may find it helpful to use a bit of imagery here. View the criticism as a parcel that is separate from either yourself or the critic. Your task is to decide whether it's a gift or a bundle of garbage.

ask questions

Questions offer the most effective strategy for dealing with criticism:

- They allow you to appear reasonable, measured, and in control even though you may be seething inside.
- They give you time to cool down. You're less likely to blow your top while you are concentrating on asking questions.

■ Asking your critic to give more specific information allows you to ascertain whether there is any substance to complaints that are couched in generalities.

■ Questions can enable you to uncover real motivation – vindictiveness masquerading as constructive comment.

■ You can put the ball back in the critic's court by asking what suggestions they have to resolve the matter.

Questions are a less inflammatory way of getting to the truth than direct challenges. Where it emerges that the critic is mistaken then they are able to back down more easily than if you had issued a direct challenge. The same applies if you are subsequently shown to be wrong. If the other person is just trying to be flippant or to put you down in some way, then asking them to give you more detail will generally cause them to back off.

seek a second opinion

If you are unsure whether a criticism is justified, seek a second opinion. Go to a person whose opinion you respect and try to approach them in a spirit of genuine enquiry, not defensiveness.

call time out

If you are feeling sensitive and vulnerable and are tempted to counter-attack, it can help to seek a postponement of the discussion rather than risk it descending into negativity. Be honest with the person making the criticism – 'I'll welcome hearing what you have to say, but I'm not feeling totally positive right now. Could we talk about it tomorrow?' Don't use this as a technique to put off criticism indefinitely.

acknowledge it

Why would you want to acknowledge criticism? Surely that's an unassertive thing to do. Well no. It doesn't have to be. Provided you do it for the right reasons, it can be an entirely assertive action. Simply acknowledging what is being said, or the part of it that is valid, without distress or defensiveness allows you to:

- disarm somebody who is trying to provoke you;
- save energy that might be wasted on a pointless argument;
- give yourself time to consider the validity of the remarks;
- take the anger out of a situation.

Acknowledging doesn't mean apologising unnecessarily or putting up with abuse. It is just about indicating that you have heard what is being said, and that perhaps there might be some validity to it. You maintain control by refusing to get emotionally roused by the criticism, but you may leave yourself the option to return to the issue when you have had a chance to consider it and you may also use acknowledgement as a prelude to some of the strategies covered earlier, such as questioning or seeking a second opinion. Here is an example of how an exchange might go:

Critic: 'I had a hell of a job understanding your presentation. Total gobbledegook!'
Respondent: 'Yes, it was a rather complex subject.'
Critic: 'It would help if you used less jargon.'
Respondent: 'Yes, there's probably too much jargon around these days. Tell me, what were the things you didn't understand?'

responding

So, you've managed to separate the accurate from the inaccurate, the constructive from the destructive. How do you respond?

If the criticism is accurate and constructive:

- acknowledge and accept the criticism with good grace;
- make any apologies that may be necessary;
- tell the other person what you are going to do to resolve the situation.

If the criticism is accurate but destructive or vindictive:

- acknowledge any mistake you have made and apologise if necessary;
- respond assertively to destructive or vindictive comments;
- take whatever steps are necessary to remedy the situation.

If you believe the criticism is inaccurate:

- ask questions to determine how the misperception may have arisen, and whether it is yours or the other person's;
- seek a second opinion if you are uncertain whether the criticism is accurate;
- correct any misperceptions.

If the criticism is both inaccurate and vindictive:

- remain calm;
- ask questions rather than making direct challenges;
- correct inaccuracies and respond to personal comments assertively;
- resist the urge to counter-attack;
- forget about the criticism.

Remember that even the most successful, competent and assertive people attract criticism. Try to use it as a tool for your own development, rather than a source of emotional upheaval and loss of self-esteem.

inviting criticism

We all have an image of ourselves that can differ markedly from the way others see us and we may go for years without hearing what people genuinely think about us. So it might seem that seeking critical feedback from others is to risk denting self-esteem. It doesn't have to be so. Provided you go about it in the right way, inviting feedback is not only an assertive thing to do, it allows you to correct misinterpretations and relieve yourself of the tension and uncertainty that occur whenever you are unsure how you are coming across.

how to seek feedback

1. Pick the right person. It needs to be someone you trust and can be relaxed with. Obviously you will want to feel that they are not the type to use the opportunity to score over you. But neither do you want to approach a sycophant who will only tell you what they think you want to hear. Go for somebody who you know deals in truth. If you approach the wrong person, you'll get the wrong answer.
2. Let the person know that you are asking them because you value their opinion. Emphasise that what you are looking for is balanced constructive criticism – that you want to know what you have done right as well as what you may have done wrong.
3. Don't just ask them out of the blue what they think of you. Most people faced with this sort of request will be startled and embarrassed, and will give you a watered down version of their real opinions. Give thought beforehand to the things you want to know about, and give them some leads. 'I'm concerned that I might be

coming over as rather distant with people in the office. Is it true?'

4. Seek specific examples of the things you have done well and not so well. Ask for practical suggestions on what you might do differently in future.

5. Having raised the points you want to hear about, listen to the responses. Don't get defensive about things that may be uncomfortable. They could be misperceptions on the part of the person you are talking to, but provided you have set up the exchange properly, they will be genuinely held ones.

combat bullying

Anyone who is the victim of bullying is liable to suffer damage to their self-esteem. The archetypal bully is somebody who picks on those they perceive to be weaker and submits them to a climate of unpredictability and fear through tantrums, intimidating behaviour, threats and humiliation. But not all bullies operate in this conveniently visible way. They may also display the sort of indirect aggression we discussed in the previous section:

■ constantly finding fault, nit-picking and criticising;
■ undermining the other person – spreading rumours, ostracising;
■ making unreasonable demands, withholding necessary resources.

We are most likely to encounter the bully in the workplace or in relationships. Workplace bullies tend to be higher in the pecking order than their victims, but this is by no means always the case. Bullying occurs between people at the same level and there are even cases of people bullying their superiors. In some professions such as education and the health service, staff may be on the receiving end of bullying clients. The classic bully is a person who has low self-esteem and uses the behaviour as an attempt to bolster their security and status at the expense of others.

There may be a second category of bully who is responding to circumstances rather than behaving in consequence of psychological problems. In an increasingly pressurised working environment such people are reacting to the demands they themselves are facing. They are stressed as a result of overload with which they can't cope and are passing the pressure down the line. Their bullying behaviour may be about unleashing some of the anger they feel in relation to the pressure they find themselves under or may arise from sheer desperation to get things done.

There is no simple answer to dealing with a bully, but one thing is certain – if you do nothing, you can look forward to continuation of the trouble with all the attendant misery and damage to your self-belief. You may have noticed that within a group some people get victimised much more frequently than others – some not at all. Those who suffer most are the ones perceived by the bully to have some area of vulnerability – perhaps they lack assertiveness, are particularly self-deprecating, have a need to feel valued. Or perhaps it is that they are different in some way to other members of the group – different tastes and views, a tendency to be more isolated.

I'm not suggesting that you seek to change your views and personality to combat bullying, but some of the strategies covered elsewhere in this book will help to prevent you becoming a victim:

- Work on being more assertive in your day-to-day dealings.
- Make yourself less dependent on the approval of others.
- Seek some alliances with like-minded individuals.

■ Don't let your body language or speech send out submissive signals. Draw yourself up to your full height, don't stoop, maintain eye contact.

■ Eliminate any self-disparaging messages from what you say. Expressions like 'Oh my views don't count for anything' almost invite people to victimise you.

facing up to the bully

Deciding whether to face up to a bully is a matter of judgement. From where I sit it's impossible to know exactly what you are faced with, so it would be irresponsible for me to make a sweeping statement such as *the only way to deal with a bully is to face up to them.* But sooner or later somebody has to, and if you are able to do it, you may be able to free yourself and raise your own self-belief in the process. There is a risk involved, but it's another of those occasions to ask yourself, 'What is the worst possible outcome?' and 'What are the alternatives?' and weigh the possible risks against the benefits.

Assuming you decide to raise the issue with the bully, it's important not to get emotional or fly off the handle. If you lose control, then the bully has achieved the power over you that they are seeking. So the name of the game is: calm, controlled and assertive:

■ Be clear in your mind beforehand what behaviour you are unhappy about.

■ Use the positive thinking and assertiveness techniques we have already mentioned – visualisation, anchoring, learning your lines, scratched record.

■ Tell the person coherently and unequivocally what they have done that you believe to be unreasonable and unfair.

■ Be specific. If you are complaining immediately following the behaviour this is straightforward, but if your complaint relates to a pattern of behaviour over time then it helps to have a record of specific instances. Don't let the bully trivialise the complaint by homing in on just one incident.

■ Be prepared for attempts to belittle your complaint or to throw it back on to you – 'You're just being silly and emotional' or 'If you can't stand the heat, get out of the kitchen.' Stand your ground. It is not your fault, it is the bully's problem and they must be made aware of it.

Even if you get through to them, don't expect instant results. You may need to return to the issue on several occasions before you see a change in attitude. But once you have summoned the courage on the first occasion, subsequent encounters tend to be less difficult. Stick to the same formula – calm and firm. Your bully is unlikely to acknowledge their behaviour, but don't confuse reaction with outcome. The reaction to your complaint may be disgruntled, offhand, puzzled or offensive, but if you notice some ensuing change then you've had an effect. Celebrate any changes, and if you feel they are really making an effort to treat you with greater respect, give some positive feedback. Even bullies respond to praise.

It is possible that the person is not aware of their bullying behaviour. Because the behaviour arises from a sense of inadequacy in the bully themself, there is a tendency towards self-deception – bullies seeing their behaviour simply as tough management or directness in a relationship. And, I have to say it, for all that bullying is a serious problem, there is a tendency on the part of some people who perceive themselves as victims to overplay the issue and to characterise criticism or justified censure as bullying. It's a convenient way of absolving themselves of responsibility. We should not underrate the damage bullying causes, but it is worth remembering that when one is feeling particularly vulnerable there may be a tendency to apply the bullying sticker, with limited justification, to behaviour that feels uncomfortable.

seeking assistance

There is no reason to regard the involvement of others as an indication of weakness on your part. Seeking some assistance is a sensible and proactive thing to do, and far preferable to enduring bullying behaviour. Simply putting up with bullying may damage more than your self-esteem. The stress it causes may have a catastrophic effect on your work performance, your health, your relationships or your home life. A sensible first step may be to share your concerns with a trusted friend or colleague. In addition to a welcome friendly ear and moral support, they may be able to help you to articulate your complaint and assist you in dealing with it more assertively. They might also have a contribution to make in identifying any behaviours on your part that make you more susceptible to bullying. Within a group, it may be that others are being similarly affected by the same person's behaviour and, if so, there could be mutual support or a possible joint approach.

workplace bullying

If you are a member of a union or professional association then it may be worthwhile discussing your complaint with them. Bullying is an issue on which all the major unions have clear policies and guidelines, and is generally regarded as a high priority for them.

An approach to management inevitably raises the level of formality, but do not be deterred by the thought that you will be considered weak and silly. There is a growing awareness of bullying and many larger companies and public organisations now have anti-bullying policies. If the person you are complaining about is your own manager, then you will need to go to the next level up, or to the human resources department if there is one. You will need to decide whether you wish to make the approach alone or to be accompanied by a friend or representative. Don't present your complaint in an apologetic manner. Remember that it is your right not to be treated in a bullying fashion. Victims of bullying who are themselves in management positions are often the most reluctant to take up a complaint formally, feeling that it is an admission of inadequacy on their part. Dismiss this notion; managers get bullied too.

Once you have taken the decision to involve a third party it is most important that you marshal your facts. Bullies often have a Jekyll and Hyde tendency – vicious in private, charming and reasonable in public – and can be consummate liars. If you find yourself reaching a formal grievance stage it could be your word against the bully's. It's important, well before it comes to that, to keep whatever records you can:

■ Keep records of incidents to which you may need to refer, including dates and times.

■ Keep copies of any correspondence that may support your case.

■ It is a good idea to document incidents that might otherwise become just anecdotal evidence. For example, if your boss has attempted to saddle you with impossible demands, send him or her a memo detailing the reasons you believe them to be unreasonable.

external advice

If your own efforts are not bearing fruit or you need advice before proceeding to more formal stages, there are a number of organisations and Web sites dedicated to providing such assistance. A good example is a site called Bully Online, which can be found at www.successunlimited.co.uk. It combines excellent advice aimed at combating bullying in all its manifestations together with an online support forum and links to other sites. The Advisory Conciliation and Arbitration Service (ACAS) offers advice leaflets on workplace bullying aimed at both employees and employers. If your health is suffering, a visit to your GP may be called for. Do not simply go on suffering alone.

conquer fears and setbacks

fears

As we have already seen, low self-esteem has a lot to do with fear – fear of making a fool of yourself, fear of being exposed as a fraud, fear of confrontation, fear of failure. Our lack of belief in ourselves leads us to exaggerate and distort the possible outcomes of our actions. We overestimate the likelihood that things will go wrong, we exaggerate the possible consequences if they do, and we underestimate our capacity to deal with the problems and difficulties we may face.

The way we most commonly respond to things that make us anxious or fearful is to avoid them. Avoidance takes various forms:

- procrastination – I'll deal with it tomorrow, next week, next month;
- pretending to ourselves – inventing good reasons why the feared activity should not be carried out;
- using other tasks as distractions to prevent us having to face up to those we are afraid of;
- using other people as props or shields.

The more we avoid those things that make us anxious, the greater the fear becomes. Initial avoidance eases our anxiety, and that leads us to employ the same strategy next time the threatening situation presents itself. And by avoiding the things that make us anxious we give ourselves no opportunity to test the validity of our fears, so the exaggerations and distortions are reinforced. With each incidence of avoidance it becomes more difficult to face up to whatever we are afraid of. We become ever more anxious, feel ever more useless and our self-esteem declines accordingly. The difficult phone call or the confrontational meeting that we have repeatedly postponed and worried about, becomes almost impossible to contemplate. We are locked into a vicious spiral of avoidance.

So, avoidance may give us a temporary feeling of relief, but it does so at the expense of a longer-term decline in self-belief. The smokescreens we throw up to disguise our lack of action don't really deceive us. We see through the excuses and condemn ourselves for our weakness. Avoidance is a strategy intended to spare ourselves pain but it isn't a pain-free solution. We simply exchange the perceived pain of facing up to our fears for the nagging and debilitating misery of guilt and self-condemnation.

All the time we engage in avoidance activity we are telling ourselves that the pain of facing our fears will be greater than the pain of avoiding them. We need to reverse that situation and perceive the pain of avoidance as being greater than the pain of facing the fear. One way of doing this is by taking account of the cumulative effect of avoidance pain. It comes in a steady drip whereas the pain of facing up to a fear is perceived as a single massive hit. But over time those constant drips of low-level distress from avoidance probably add up to far more discomfort than the activity that is being avoided.

And what about our perception of the pain involved in facing the fear? As we have already seen, avoidance serves to exaggerate the original fear. We get it out of proportion. When we finally do pluck up the courage to do something we have repeatedly postponed, not only is there a massive release from the pain of avoidance, but frequently we find that the feared activity turns out to be nowhere near as bad as we had imagined it to be. It's rather like removing a sticking plaster. Seeking to avoid pain by gently pulling on it results in far greater discomfort than summoning up the courage to whip it off.

All of this leads to the inescapable conclusion that the only way to deal with fears is to face up to them. Let's take a look at how we might do that.

ask yourself some questions

Questions are a good way of reducing the irrationality and disproportion that tends to come about when we allow fears to rampage unchecked. Ask yourself:

- What exactly am I afraid of?
- Why am I inclined to avoid it?
- In what ways might I be exaggerating or distorting the scale of the challenge?
- What will I lose by not tackling it?
- What similar challenges have I successfully tackled in the past?
- What resources can I draw upon to help me tackle it?
- If I face up to this fear, what is the worst thing that can happen to me?
- What will I gain by facing up to this fear?
- How will I feel after I have faced up to it?
- How will facing up to it help me the next time I have a similar challenge?

recognise that it's OK to be afraid

Fears are made worse for many of us because we fear the very sensation of fear. We don't want to put ourselves in situations where we will encounter that sense of apprehension and discomfort and so we stick doggedly to those things that we know will not put us in danger of it. But the experiences that make us afraid may also have the potential to offer us the greatest amounts of achievement and fulfilment, and the apprehension we feel before embarking upon them should be part of gearing ourselves up to give of our best. Most actors, entertainers and sportspeople will testify to the fact that a certain degree of fear is a prerequisite to a really great performance. It's a matter of getting the balance right – a level of apprehension that brings out the best we have to offer and does not tip us into avoidance and paralysis. So, don't be frightened to feel the fear, but keep it in balance by using some of the other techniques covered in this section.

present yourself with graded challenges

Wherever it is possible to do so, adopt a gradual approach to confronting your fears. It's possible that jumping in at the deep end may help some people to swim, but it's more likely to terrify them to the point that they never want to go near the water again. So your first stage in facing up to a feared activity should be to set yourself a challenge that introduces a degree of anxiety, but isn't so scary that you are unable to tackle it. If you are scared of speaking up at meetings, then you might set yourself the target of just asking one question, or making one simple point. Reward yourself for achieving this, and stick with the same level of participation until you feel comfortable with it, and then raise the bar. Set yourself a new level, reward yourself, stick with it until comfortable and raise the bar again. It won't always be a constant upward curve. There will be setbacks, but provided you keep setting yourself achievable challenges and rewarding yourself immediately for overcoming them, the overall trend will be upwards.

prepare to be positive

Some of the challenges you may fear are not amenable to the 'one step at a time' treatment. If, for example, you are scared of situations involving confrontation and are faced with having to make a complaint or deal with a difficult interpersonal issue, then the sort of gradualist approach I have described above won't get you too far. It's an all or nothing situation and, if you are going to tackle it, you need to take the bull by the horns. In such circumstances you can very usefully draw upon some of the techniques we looked at earlier.

Visualisation allows you to rehearse the feared situation in a relaxed and controlled manner before the event. It gives you the chance to deal with those subsidiary concerns that are so much a part of presenting yourself confidently and authoritatively to other people – questions like 'Will I be able to say what I mean? Will I keep control of my emotions?' As you run the visualisation, picture yourself dealing with the situation, hear the words that you are using, and inwardly listen to the sound of your own voice – measured and assured. Make sure that you are relaxed and comfortable before you start the visualisation and be prepared to run it several times for maximum benefit.

Anchoring offers you the support of previous positive experience when you most need it. You can build yourself an anchor that will help you out when you have to tackle a situation that makes you anxious or afraid.

The tendency to feed ourselves negative messages is most acute with those things that make us anxious or afraid. The prospect of tackling your fears becomes overwhelming if you are simultaneously filling your head with statements such as, 'I'm never going to manage this. It's too scary. Might as well give up now.' It's most important to approach feared activities in a positive frame of mind. If you think you can't do it then you can't. But just as negative self-talk diminishes your ability to act, positive affirmations can boost it. Cultivate enabling beliefs and consciously eliminate the negative messages, replacing them with simple constructive statements of encouragement.

reverse the order
Arrange your list of things to do with those tasks you fear at

the top of the list and the ones you enjoy most at the bottom. Tackle the list in order, and not only do you get the relief that comes from overcoming challenges that otherwise might be postponed, but also you are rewarded with successively more attractive tasks as you work your way down the list.

go for immediacy

When you have resolved to tackle something that makes you anxious, get on with it as soon as possible. The longer you leave it, the more you will find yourself inventing excuses, allowing the fear to grow or re-establish itself. If you have decided to speak up at a meeting, say something early on, even if it is just to ask a question. Rather like the goalkeeper's early touch of the ball in a football match, it gives your confidence a lift that helps when you come to be more severely tested. Where the activity you fear is not one that you can deal with immediately, at least do something that commits you: arrange an appointment or schedule a time when you will deal with it.

hang on to the feeling

Remember how it felt when you did it. It is very important to hang on to that sense of relief and accomplishment that follows from successfully confronting a situation that made you anxious. Remember how different it feels from the temporary relief of avoidance. Note also how situations seldom turn out to be as difficult as you had feared. Log all these thoughts and feelings in your memory bank – or even better commit them to paper in your diary – so you can draw on them if you are tempted to bottle out of a frightening situation in future.

whose fears are they, anyway?

They are yours, of course. You are the one who created them, and they don't exist anywhere other than inside your head. So, take ownership of them and recognise that what you have made you can overcome. Once you have made this attitude shift it is harder to invent excuses or to see your fears as insurmountable blocks placed in your way. Standing up to them becomes a matter of motivation rather than ability.

failures

Of all the fears that nibble away at our self-esteem, the fear of failure is the most pernicious. It leads us to avoid challenges, to steer clear of anything that might involve risk, or to give up at the first sign of difficulty. At its most extreme it paralyses us. We wait until we can be assured of success before we are prepared to make a move. Such certainty is never forthcoming, and as a consequence we venture nothing, achieve nothing, feel bad about ourselves and spend our lives bemoaning what might have been.

Now I'm sure this extreme description does not fit you, but there is a little of it in most of us. So let's take a few minutes to consider the fear of failure and how we can work to overcome it.

Failure carries a very personal label. Our fear is that if we try something and fail, we will be in some way less worthy as human beings. We see ourselves not as people who have experienced failure but as failures per se. It's easy to see why. The pass/fail axe has been dangled over our lives since childhood. Passing the test offers a gateway to whatever we have set out to do while failure leaves us out in the cold. And it's true that people are conveniently labelled 'successes' or 'failures'. But isn't it ironic that in an effort to avoid the failure label we shrink from the very challenges that could lead to success? All the time that we sit in our comfort zones and dream, we can convince ourselves that we have the potential to succeed. Our fear is that, as soon as we set foot outside and put ourselves to the test, we will be found wanting.

The truth is that everyone experiences failure at some time and that it is those who do not fear it who are able to learn from it and move on. In order to win, you must dare to lose, and that means stepping outside the comfort zone.

Your comfort zone is that range of experiences and activities in your life that is safe and familiar and within which you are not unduly distressed by risk, challenge and uncertainty. Naturally, the range of activities will differ greatly from person to person, but what is often overlooked is the fact that it varies over time for the same individual. Think back. Can you recall activities that once had you cringing with apprehension, but now are things you can take in your stride? Or more worryingly, are there challenges that once seemed a breeze, but are now sources of considerable anxiety? The comfort zone is capable of expansion, but most importantly, if we don't constantly push at its boundaries it will shrink – our confidence diminishes and there is a smaller and smaller range of activities with which we feel comfortable. The effect is not unlike that arising from lack of physical exercise. Just as an armchair lifestyle makes muscles weak and flabby, so a comfort zone existence weakens our resolve. By stepping outside the comfort zone and pushing to the limits of our capabilities, not only do we give of our best, but we also commonly find that activities we feared are not too threatening after all, and they become part of an expanded zone of comfort. Of course, stepping outside the comfort zone involves the possibility of failure, but only by risking failure can you experience the success. At the end of the day, staying locked inside the comfort zone is not a particularly comfortable thing to do.

So, the question is how far and how often to step outside it. One way of looking at the issue is to view the environment in which you operate as consisting of three concentric circles (see Figure 8.1). The innermost of these is your comfort zone – those activities that present you with no threat and with limited stress. Beyond this is your stretch zone – activities and experiences that do put you under pressure but where the effect is empowering rather than debilitating. It is by moving out into the stretch zone that growth occurs. You give yourself new

challenges, meet them, and what was formerly part of your
stretch zone becomes part of a new, broader comfort zone. You
don't have to spend all your time in the stretch zone – we all
need a certain amount of the familiar, the routine, the safe – but
it's important to stretch yourself for some of the time.

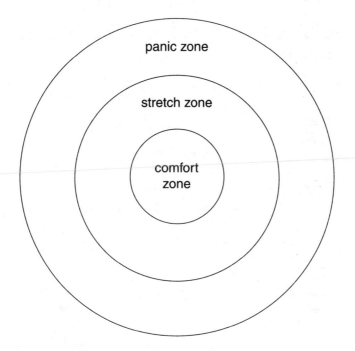

Figure 8.1 *Beyond the comfort zone*

The outermost circle is your panic zone – the point at which
increased pressure has a detrimental effect on performance –
and it is to be avoided. But as with the other two zones, there
are no fixed boundaries to your panic zone. The more you are
able to rise to challenges and broaden your comfort zone, the
further you will extend the boundary of panic. It's back to my
earlier point about giving yourself graded challenges and
banking your successes.

Despite everything that has been said so far, there will be occasions when you perceive yourself to have failed. The point to hang on to is not 'I must not fail,' but 'I must not be afraid of failing.' Failure is not the end of the world. You can get up and try again. Let's look at how.

it looks like failure, feels like failure, therefore...

Not necessarily. What we judge to be failure on our own part may not be so. There are a variety of reasons why we get it wrong:

■ We draw conclusions based on our feelings. In situations like interviews and presentations where we are required to perform in front of others, we interpret our feelings of self-consciousness harshly. The reasoning goes: 'I felt like an idiot, therefore I must be an idiot, and it goes without saying that I made a mess of the task.'

■ We don't receive the feedback we expect. Those of us with low self-esteem tend to be heavily dependent on feedback from others to tell us when we have done well. For all sorts of reasons we may not get what we expect. The people we look to for feedback may be preoccupied with other things, unskilled at providing feedback, concerned to bolster their own self-esteem at our expense or just simply unobservant. Or it may be that we are expecting too much from others.

■ We set excessively high standards for ourselves – often higher than we would dream of setting for others. We find faults where they hardly exist and may have a habit of exaggerating out of all proportion small flaws that we wouldn't notice in someone else's performance.

▓ What constitutes a failure will depend on expectations. Two students achieve an upper second-class degree. The first is delighted because he was not expecting to do well. The second is devastated because she was hoping for a first. This is not to say that you should avoid high expectations, just be sure they are not wholly unrealistic. And be prepared for the fact that the closer you go to the limit of your capabilities the more likely it is that there will be occasions when you don't quite make it. Get the thing in proportion. Aiming high and at times not quite achieving your goal has to be better than aiming low and churning out meaningless successes.

Of course, not all our setbacks are the result of misperceptions or exaggerations. We will all face numerous reverses that are unequivocal. But however clear the setback, the sense of failure is still largely of our own making. Even when we have suffered a genuine setback, we are unable to view it as a challenge to start afresh or to change our behaviour, but take it to be something wrong with ourselves. The urge not to repeat the experience is an attempt to reduce the future incidence of failure, but taken to its extreme such a strategy would result in us never taking any risks and never trying anything new – a state of affairs clearly not conducive to any form of achievement, and totally destructive of self-belief. On the other hand, it makes no sense pointlessly to set yourself up for failure. So we need a strategy that both reduces the incidence of unnecessary setbacks and provides us with the resources to deal with them positively when they do occur. Here are some ways to achieve it.

how to overcome setbacks

balance aspiration and realism
As discussed in Chapter 5, goals need to be stretching but

achievable. If you make your goals impossibly high or expect to reach them in one leap, then you set yourself up for failure. However, it is perfectly acceptable to have a target that is well out of reach provided you put in place sub-goals – graduated steps that will enable you to experience a sense of progress as you make your way towards it. As with your goals, don't set performance standards that are too perfectionist. Without settling for sub-standard, don't judge the occasional lapse too harshly.

trust your own judgement
Too often we are over-reliant on other people's judgement of what constitutes a successful performance. Does the fact that only one of Van Gogh's masterpieces was sold in his lifetime make them any less worthy? Wherever possible, make your measures of achievement independent of other people's judgement or your perceptions of their judgement. With a job interview, for example, step back from the result and look objectively at how you dealt with the questions, not whether the selectors chose you. This approach not only frees you from over-reliance on the estimation of others, but gives you a more positive lead into examining what you might do differently in future.

don't pursue success at all costs
Of course you should aim for success and celebrate it, but if success is the only thing that matters, then the pain and disappointment of setbacks will be much harder to bear. Concentrate on the process and not just the prize. Take satisfaction in getting the details of what you are doing right, and reward yourself for tackling obstacles that may be thrown in your path along the way.

record the setbacks that you overcome
It's an unfortunate fact that one failure can wipe out a whole string of successes. And we are more likely to remember the

disasters than the occasions when we battled our way through setbacks and disappointments. When you are facing a difficult challenge, one of the most valuable things you can have in your armoury is the recollection of successfully dealing with a problem that was in some way similar in the past. It provides a reference you can draw upon that leads you to believe that you can make a success of the new challenge.

I strongly recommend that you use your diary to record challenges overcome and achievements, however small. Use it also to register the steps you will take to bounce back from setbacks and disappointments. Setting these things down on paper helps you to adopt a problem-solving approach and gives a sense of commitment. And at times of future difficulty you have a record that proves you are able to build yourself back up from even the toughest of reverses.

remember that failure can make you stronger.

It would be nice to think that we can hit the bulls-eye every time, but unfortunately it isn't going to happen. We all fail some time. Failure offers the opportunity to rethink, to learn and to begin again. If you come out of it in the right frame of mind, it can be an opportunity to do things a lot better. Failure should be a chance to sharpen your resolve, not an excuse for giving up – failure actually makes you stronger. And at risk of repeating myself, don't forget that it is only when the chips are down that we really produce our best.

mistakes

Just as we all fail from time to time, so we all make mistakes. And once again it's something we fear. We are afraid of the response we may receive if our mistakes become known – ridicule, loss of status, humiliation – and so we resort to concealment, diversion or self-condemnation:

■ We cover up our errors in the hope that they won't be discovered.

■ We absolve ourselves of responsibility by self-justification or seeking to blame others.

■ We subject ourselves to disproportionate punishment by exaggerating the effects of the mistake and dwelling on it far longer than necessary.

All of these strategies are destructive of healthy self-esteem. Self-justification might appear to be protective of self-belief, but it is often a pretence that convinces neither ourselves nor others. Clearly none of us will set out deliberately to make mistakes, but when they do occur, our self-esteem is best served if we are able openly to acknowledge them, learn from them and then move on.

acknowledging mistakes

It's something of a paradox, but acknowledging a mistake can actually make you feel better about yourself than trying to cover it up. Although the impulse to conceal or deny is a protective one, you are more likely to maintain your own self-respect and receive the respect of others if you are open and honest. And don't forget that concealment uncovered almost inevitably does more damage than the original error. By owning up you are saying to yourself and others, 'Yes, I'm like everyone else. I do make mistakes, and I'm brave enough to deal with them.' You are also preparing the ground for learning and moving on. This is impossible to do all the time you seek to conceal or deny.

learning and moving on

In Chapter 3 we examined the common tendency to revisit even quite minor mistakes, often for weeks afterwards, repeatedly chastising oneself and looking at how the error might have been avoided. This does your self-esteem no good at all. It's important that you learn any necessary lessons and then achieve closure, and one way to achieve this is by adopting a form of self-counselling role using your diary or notebook as the vehicle. Write down what you felt about the mistake at the time and ask yourself how you would expect to respond differently if such a situation presented itself in the future. Be sure to look forward. Simply raking over the debris is not the way to do it. So don't ask, 'Where did I go wrong?' Reframe the question as 'What will I do differently in future?' Express what you have learned in positive terms and forgive yourself the error. Then mentally stamp the issue 'Dealt with' and consign it to the archives.

Everything that I have said here about setbacks, failure and mistakes cannot take away the fact that they all hurt. They don't have to result in self-condemnation, loss of self-belief and retirement from the fray, but they still sting. As with any injuries, they may need a bit of nursing. So don't expect that you will always be able to bounce back immediately. But the sooner you start to take action, the quicker you'll recover, and the less chance there is of negative influences getting to work. So don't wallow in the hurt. Allow yourself as short a recovery time as is reasonable, before you start to turn things around.

balance your life

One of the recurrent themes in this book has been that of maintaining balance. I have suggested that you should:

- strive for excellence but avoid the downside of perfectionism;
- boost your self-acceptance but maintain an honest appraisal of your strengths and weaknesses;
- find the right level of pressure to get the best out of yourself without tipping over into avoidance and paralysis;
- enjoy success but don't make it the only thing that matters;
- set ambitious targets but be sure they are achievable.

In this penultimate chapter I would like to look at a further balancing act that is important to maintaining healthy levels of self-esteem: achieving a balanced lifestyle.

a balanced lifestyle

Why is a balanced lifestyle important for self-esteem? Well, firstly because over-concentration on one or two areas of our lives is liable to leave us feeling unfulfilled – less than rounded human beings. Those other things we have wanted to do with our lives are endlessly consigned to the back burner, and the 'if onlys' and 'should haves' start to feature in our thoughts. And overemphasis of one area may have a directly detrimental consequence for another – health and relationships are an obvious casualty of excessive working hours.

A further consequence may be that our self-image is unhealthily associated with one single aspect of our lives. It may be that we come to view our worth solely in terms of our work or our family role. When this is the case, the effect of that role ending can be devastating. A job is declared redundant, a marriage ends, children grow up and leave home, retirement looms – all self-esteem disasters from which it may be difficult to recover.

The major focus of balance tends to be upon work – either in respect of excessive hours that preclude other activity or the ability of individuals to maintain paid employment alongside other demanding roles as parents, carers or people for whom health issues may limit ability to undertake traditional work patterns. Let's spend a little time looking at the main work/life balance issues and what you may do to address them.

Maintaining a healthy balance of activity in your life has been likened to juggling. You are trying to keep five balls in the air: work, family and relationships, health, leisure and personal growth. Some of them are rubber balls and some glass. The trick is to distinguish which is which. Too often we treat work as if it were glass when it could really be rubber.

are you working too many hours?

In many work environments excessive hours are an issue – the 60-hour week is almost a badge of office in some. But it's seldom the case that nothing can be done about it. You may want to think about: managing your time better, prioritising your work, streamlining the way you handle information, learning to say no to unimportant tasks, controlling interruptions. My book *Organising Yourself* – also part of the Creating Success series – may be of some help if you wish to explore these issues.

is work invading the rest of your life?

For many it's not just a matter of working excessive hours, but of allowing work to invade the whole of our lives. We bring work home at evenings and weekends. We may postpone tackling it but it remains there, a looming presence, and we are never mentally free of it. Our whole life timetable is structured around work. This is a particular problem for the self-employed and the increasing numbers of us who work from home, but it's also an issue for all those whose hours of employment have no easily defined limits. If you are affected, you may need to take radical action to set boundaries on the times when you will work and be disciplined in ensuring that you stay within them. And, though I hate to suggest it, you may also need to adopt a more structured approach to family and leisure time to protect your quality of life and defend it against the all-encroaching work.

are you in the right job?

Many of us remain for years in jobs that are unfulfilling, unsuited to our talents or even downright damaging to our self-esteem. Alternatively we may be in jobs that are intrinsically satisfying but prevent us achieving some of the other things we want to do. If either of these is the case for you, it may be time to ask yourself some hard questions about what you really want from your working life and how much you are prepared to do in order to get it. How important is your current level of income to you? People who take the plunge into a different career will generally have to be prepared for a period of financial belt-tightening. How important is your existing status? Some are shocked to find it means more to them than they realise. Could you keep your options open, or plan a phased move into the new activity, possibly by starting out on a spare time basis? Be sure that you have adequately thought through all the implications of change and take any reasonable steps to confirm that the grass really is greener on the other side of the valley. Whatever you do to change your employment situation there will be risks involved. But how does a spell of insecurity compare against a lifetime of regret for missed opportunities? It's a matter of minimising the avoidable uncertainty and accepting the unavoidable. If we wait for a time when we can be absolutely certain that our actions will lead to success, then we will wait forever.

do you want a different working arrangement?

Perhaps your need is for a more flexible or part-time working arrangement to allow more time for the other important elements of your life. Employers are increasingly becoming aware that flexible working arrangements can offer benefits in terms of more committed staff, lower turnover and better retention of expertise. But if you're thinking of approaching your employer with a proposal for a different working arrangement, it's important to do your homework first. Be sure to think about the advantages that your proposal may offer your employer and possible solutions to any difficulties that may arise from it. Here are some of the sort of questions you should ask yourself:

▓ How might your proposal assist the business or service you are providing? Could increased flexibility on hours mean that you were able to deal more effectively with pressure points in the working week or the working year? Could you offer to work longer hours at busy times and take time off during quieter periods?

▇ How might your proposal benefit the allocation of resources? Could working from home assist with pressures on workspace, for example?

▇ If your reason for wanting a new working arrangement is a desire to pursue development opportunities, might there be a pay-off in terms of additional skills and knowledge you would be able to bring to the job?

▇ Might it be possible for part of your current job to be carried out by somebody at a more junior level, thus saving money for the employer as well as freeing you for part of the week?

▇ How are other members of staff likely to view your proposal? Could it give rise to any jealousies or requests from others that might not be sustainable? What sort of consultation might be needed?

▇ What would be the effect of your proposal on the service you provide? Are there things that you would not be able to do, and if so, how would they be achieved? Would it be necessary for you to make any special arrangements for cover or contact at times you are not present?

do you need to increase the work element?

For some, the balance issue is not one of reducing the time spent on work, but increasing it. For those who have taken a career break for family or other reasons, or those who might have been away from the workplace by reason of extended illness or unemployment, the route back into employment can be a major self-esteem issue. Again it's a matter requiring some clear thinking and planning. Recognise that for almost every-body moving back into employment there is a significant confidence hurdle to be overcome, but most people tend to overestimate the scale of the challenge.

It may appear that the job has moved on a long way during the time you have been out of the fray. There may be new processes, new jargon and new technology, all of which can appear highly confusing. But you will often find that apparently radical changes are not nearly as great as they at first seem, and that underlying competencies remain pretty much unchanged. Ask yourself questions such as:

- ▓ What skills do I need to update?
- ▓ What skills are still relevant?
- ▓ How will I get the updating I need? Are there opportunities to acquire it informally through contacts I have through my former employment, or will I need to consider some formal retraining?
- ▓ Could there be a part-time or freelance route back to paid employment?

Consider also whether you have gained any useful new skills during the period that you have been away from paid employment. Be prepared to think creatively here and don't undersell yourself. People who have been involved in caring roles, for example, may develop a range of skills and insights, both in their main capacity and through other voluntary activities, and these may be useful in people-related employment. If so, take the trouble to identify and market these attributes.

Finally, recognise that change may have been as tough for those who have remained within the job as it is for you. They have had the additional burden of those changes that came and went during the time you were away.

a healthy balance

There is no doubt that health and fitness has a significant bearing on self-esteem. I hardly need to make the point that how we view ourselves is going to be affected by how well we look after our bodies. I'm not talking here about the extremes of physical concern – the obsessive focus on body shape and appearance that we discussed earlier in the book – but a common sense approach to eating well, getting enough exercise and taking care of our appearance. The self-esteem benefits of being fitter and healthier come in the form of:

- improved body image;
- greater range of physical activity within your grasp;
- reduced levels of stress and anxiety;
- improved stamina for tackling the normal activities of your day.

In the pressurised lifestyle so many of us lead these days, the two health maintenance issues most regularly sacrificed are exercise and eating a healthy balanced diet. As a nation we increasingly ride everywhere, fuel up on junk food, and then wonder why our bodies don't match up to our expectations of them.

If you are one of the many who tell themselves that they don't have time to cook good meals or to exercise, then you need to snap out of it. You are presenting yourself with excuses. Nobody is so busy that they can't spare a small amount of time to look after themselves. There are scores of great-tasting nutritious meals that can be prepared just as quickly as the fat-laden junk food alternatives. If you're stumped for ideas, try consulting one of the recent crop of recipe books aimed specifically at busy people. *Fresh Food Fast* from BBC Books offers 200 recipes and ideas that it claims can be prepared in 15 minutes or less. And there are a number of inexpensive paperbacks along the same lines. Try *Real Fast Food* by Nigel Slater or *Great Fast Food* by Gary Rhodes.

So, that's food taken care of; now what about exercise? When you don't have time for all the things you are currently supposed to be doing, and the pressure on your working day doesn't look like declining, how do you manage to fit in some physical activity? Well, 20 to 30 minutes of vigorous activity three or four times a week is all you need. Here are six ways to make sure you get it:

1. *Change your attitude.* If the thought of exercise fills you with dread, it's going to use up more of your time than necessary. We are all inclined to waste time putting off things we don't want to do. Remove this tendency by changing the way you view exercise. Vary your activities to maintain interest. Focus on the sense of well-being rather than the discomfort. Introduce a social element into exercise for greater enjoyment, and don't use exercise as a form of punishment session to remove guilt about overindulging.

2. *Develop some habits.* There are things you do every day and barely think about. If you make exercise one of these – as much a part of your daily routine as cleaning your teeth – you will cut down on planning and preparation time. Irregular exercisers are constantly having to remotivate themselves to start up again. Make exercise a priority in your day, not something that can be dropped whenever time gets tight. Scheduling it at regular times will help, but don't become too rigid or obsessive.

3. *Commute smarter.* If you live reasonably close to your workplace, then walking, cycling or running may offer significant daily exercise during time when you would otherwise be sitting in traffic. The biggest difficulty is what to do with your clothes and any paperwork or equipment you normally transport between home and

work. A specialist running rucksack or cycle panniers may be the answer, or perhaps you can make an arrangement with a colleague who lives nearby and is prepared to transport clothing and equipment for you. If you travel to work by public transport, consider getting off at an earlier stop and walking the remaining distance.

4. *Grab all opportunities.* Opportunities for sustained aerobic activity during the working day are limited, but other forms of beneficial exercise, such as stretching, can be done anywhere and at any time. Stretching reduces stress and fatigue, fosters mental alertness, improves circulation and flexibility, and prepares the body for other physical activity. Utilising the exercise potential of everyday activities can also pay dividends. Use stairs rather than lifts wherever possible and whenever your work takes you to another building, walk briskly rather than strolling. This may not seem like the foundation of super fitness, but every little helps.

5. *Make use of breaks.* Fitting your exercise into natural breaks helps you to approach the next stage in your day with renewed vigour. For too many of us, lunch consists of a sandwich snatched at our desks. If this applies to you, perhaps you could think about taking a proper break and combining it with some exercise – a brisk walk, jog, swim or gym session if facilities are available. Take the exercise before you eat and be realistic about what it is possible to fit into your lunch break. If you find yourself scampering back to your desk bathed in perspiration, then some of the benefits will be lost.

If you are in the habit of working in the evening, try scheduling an exercise session as the last activity of your working day – no more work to be done after this point. It makes an excellent boundary between work and relaxation, and prevents the tendency for your work to drift later and later into the evening.

6. *Set fitness targets*. Many of the benefits of exercise are too long-term to provide day-to-day motivation. Working to a target raises the importance of your regular exercise sessions and provides a yardstick against which to measure progress. The choice of target will depend on you and your current level of fitness – it should be challenging but achievable. Beware of setting timescales that are too ambitious. Injury is a frequent consequence of exercise pro-grammes that are increased too rapidly. A weekly increase in activity of no more than 10 per cent is often presented as a rule of thumb.

If you need others around you to provide motiva-tion, then join a group, class or gym or participate in some form of competitive activity. But if you are happy to work alone, you may cut out time spent making arrangements and travelling. Many solitary exercisers claim that work problems fall into place and new ideas emerge while they are working out alone.

One final word of caution. If you are overweight, have been inactive for a long time or have any history of heart trouble, talk to your doctor before commencing an exercise programme.

encourage others

Genuine self-esteem should be a matter not just of self-protection but of respect and consideration for others. Having devoted the previous chapters to looking after ourselves, it's appropriate that we give some final attention to helping to develop the self-esteem of others.

There are obviously altruistic reasons why you might want to encourage the self-esteem of those around you, but there are selfish reasons too. By helping others, you are developing a climate of mutuality and you will receive the returns that come from an environment of honesty, assertiveness and support.

strategies for encouraging others

So how do you set about it? Well, not surprisingly, much of what you can do to help others is about employing the same strategies that we have looked at in relation to ourselves.

encourage self-reliance

Let's be honest, we all like to feel needed. We are pleased and reassured when our children, our colleagues and our friends look to us for advice and support. But there is a line that can be all too easily crossed into territory where we encourage unhealthy levels of dependency. It may be crossed for the most caring or selfish of motives. Here are some of the ways you may impede self-reliance in others:

- completing tasks for others rather than passing on the expertise that will allow them to be more self-sufficient;
- belittling another's efforts, perhaps as a way of boosting your own self-esteem;
- adopting a controlling attitude towards those around you;
- seeking to protect others from some of the hardships of life;
- allowing defeatist and self-deprecating remarks made by others to go unchallenged;
- as a parent or manager, giving inadequate rules or guidelines;
- creating a climate of fear or uncertainty in which those around you feel unable to make any move without your approval;
- adopting a blaming approach towards mistakes.

It is not always easy to recognise these tendencies in yourself. We all have entrenched ways of behaving that we have ceased to notice, but which may have a significant effect on others. Do give the above list some thought, and possibly ask a trusted friend whether any of the items apply to you. By now, your self-esteem should be able to cope with the answers.

Encouraging greater self-reliance in others has a positive spin-off for you. You are spared the constant drain of always being the one with the answers, and you will have more confident and fulfilled people around you. In demonstrating your trust and belief in others, you will be repaid by the increased trust they show in you. If you are a manager, the effectiveness of your team could be considerably increased. But you have to be prepared for some changes to your way of operating. It means:

- being prepared to see things done in a way you would not have done them;
- allowing people to make mistakes and to learn from them without always feeling that they will be hauled over the coals;
- seeing your friends, colleagues and loved ones fail from time to time.

accept unconditionally

Don't expect others to mould themselves into the shape you wish them to be. Just as you should be prepared to accept yourself as a human being with flaws and eccentricities, so you should do the same for others. Accepting others as they are doesn't mean that you have to submerge your own views or refrain from dealing honestly and assertively with disagreements, problems and errors. But it does mean that you should resist any temptation to attach conditions to your respect for them as fellow human beings.

help people value themselves

Keep your eyes open for the achievements of others and draw attention to the things they may be in danger of taking for granted. Pick up on specific points that might otherwise pass unnoticed and help them to reframe self-deprecating remarks. Be alive to instances of self-denying behaviour – the colleague who always puts in excessive hours without complaint, the partner who submerges his or her needs in order to accommodate yours. It is so easy for such behaviour to become so well established that it is taken for granted by all concerned.

be interested

Short of bullying and abuse, few things hit an individual's self-esteem harder than receiving the impression that they don't count for anything. Taking the time to listen to people, consulting them, asking their advice – all send out the message that they matter. It's no more than good interpersonal skills, and it benefits you in terms of better communication, additional insights and greater understanding. But it's remarkably easy in our hectic lives to neglect this basic human interaction.

give genuine support and feedback

It's never easy. What you mean to be constructive and helpful may be perceived as unjust criticism or unwelcome intrusion. Be aware of this possibility, but don't seek to deal with it by engaging in elaborate preliminaries that may dilute or even negate the message you want to get across. Consider your timing, and try to catch the other person when they will be most receptive to what you have to say:

1. *Make praise genuine and specific.* General praise thrown around willy-nilly is not a lot of value. A person with low self-esteem is liable to dismiss it as mere social niceness. It will be more meaningful if you are able to notice something the other person has done and comment on it specifically.
2. *Be proximate.* Feedback is best delivered as soon after the event as possible. If what you have to say is positive then it will have a far more potent effect on motivation and performance. If the message is a critical one, then leaving it too long smacks of harbouring bad feeling and the person receiving it is more likely to interpret it as an attack.
3. *Be precise and constructive in your criticism.* Often, as givers of feedback, we hide behind vague comments

that are difficult to challenge but also impossible to unpack. These are not helpful at all. The receiver needs to know precisely what you perceive as not working well so that they can do something about it.

4. *Deal with what is achievable.* For all of us there are limits to how far and how fast we are able to change. So be sure to give people things they can get hold of. Don't just present them with a distant pinnacle. Instead, show them steps that they can take from where they are now. It's no different from the technique we looked at in relation to your own goals. Don't load them down with too many points either. It will have the same effect as expecting too much and is liable to be disheartening.

5. *Tell them what you see.* Feedback should be your honest impression of the other person's behaviour, which they may choose to accept or reject. It should not be an attempt by you to get inside their head and analyse their motives. Recognise this in what you say. For example, rather than telling someone, 'Your heart wasn't in this task,' say, 'It appeared to me as if your heart wasn't in this task.'

6. *Deal with the behaviour, not the person.* If you are giving feedback that may be interpreted as critical, be sure that you are focusing on just the behaviour in question and not making general disparaging remarks about the person. Avoid any tendency towards stereotyping, labelling or unfavourable comparisons. So it's OK to tell someone that you don't think they put enough effort into a task, but not to give them a general 'You're lazy' label or to ask, 'Why can't you be more hardworking, like Steve?'

7. *Don't indulge in negative asides.* In our cynical age, straight praise and positive feedback is not always easy to express. So we cover our discomfort with little asides and clumsy jokes that can negate everything

positive we are trying to put over. We say things like 'That was a good piece of work. I don't know who was more surprised, me or you.'

aid recovery

Recognise that everyone makes mistakes from time to time and that a knee-jerk blaming reaction is seldom helpful. Assist others in learning from errors and setbacks and in developing strategies for the future. But be sure that the recovery is theirs and not a case of you riding in with the cavalry.

end note

The suggestions and activities in the preceding chapters should provide all the ammunition you need to bring about a genuine enhancement of your self-esteem. But they will require effort and conviction on your part. You will need to work at them and be prepared to go the distance. It's not a case of employing a few quick tricks that will bring about an immediate and permanent transformation. There will always be new challenges to your self-belief and some of them will be tough. There will be occasions when it seems that you are going backwards, and not all of the techniques will work for you all of the time. But don't let yourself be blown off course. With a little perseverance you can achieve major positive changes in attitude and belief that will have a beneficial impact on everything you do. You really can feel good about yourself, enjoy your successes and handle whatever life may throw at you.

Go for it!